REFLECTIONS OF GRACE

CHRIST-LIKE MEN & WOMEN WHO INFLUENCED MY LIFE

A Memoir

Allen D. Ferry

Cover Photograph Credit: Michelle Weber

Michelle was a young member of Calvary Baptist Church in the 1990's.
She has become an excellent photographer!
More importantly, she is a honorable wife and mother.

Foreword

I have written this book to encourage another generation of men and women to consider vocational ministry.

In his book, *The Vanishing Ministry in the 21st Century: Calling a New Generation to Lifetime Service,* author Dr. Woodrow Kroll details the parental and social causes behind the diminishing number of young people who are entering vocational ministry.

Since I read his book in the 1990's, I have intentionally sought to motivate those in my circle of influence toward ministry.

I acknowledge that I have had a greater variety of ministry than most. Pastoral, military, institutional, and educational ministry opportunities await for serious-minded servants.

I hope this memoir will motive a new generation to sense the Lord's leading into these rewarding ministries.

Dedication

To my wife Theresa

To Mark & Heather, and Julaine

To my grandsons: Corban, Christian, and Enoch

To all the influential men and women noted in this book

To the men and women in uniform who stand prepared to defend our freedoms

To all the incarcerated men who have enriched my life

To all the students of Mount Olive Bible College, I'm especially grateful for your friendship and testimony.

PREFACE

My mother's father was born in 1868, my grandmother Hulda (pictured with author) was born in 1890. They were born in Sweden but later migrated to a Swedish community in northwestern Pennsylvania. They are buried nearby in Mt. Tabor cemetery.

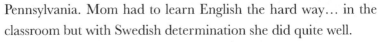

Mom was born in 1912.

When Mom was in eighth grade, her parents moved to Warren, Pennsylvania. Mom had to learn English the hard way... in the classroom but with Swedish determination she did quite well.

Dad was born in Crown, Pennsylvania but later moved to Warren. How Dad and Mom met is a mystery. They were married in 1938.

Linda, my one sibling, was born on July 14, 1940. With the onset of WWII, my parents decided to postpone my important arrival until after the war. I was born on October 7, 1947.

My sister and I conclude that connections with Swedish-speaking friends led Mom to the Bethlehem Covenant Church in Warren. For years this church had both English and Swedish services because in the early days the members were mostly Swedish.

Mom and Dad made sure that I was regularly in church. I participated in Sunday school where I learned Bible stories and memorized scripture. However, something was missing, but at that point I did not understand what it was.

CONTENT

PART ONE

EARLY LIFE

1947–1965

WARREN, PENNSYLVANIA, 1947-1965

Like most people, I was born at a very early age! Two early memories included a painful encounter with a dentist and a much better hospital experience of tonsil surgery because Mom and Dad rewarded me with a milkshake!

LAUGH WITH ME — *My sister and I have one "bloody" memory from Elm Street. Tinkertoy stems came in a tube but we were using it for a telescope between our eyes. I decided to release it just as Linda pulled it toward herself. The tube hit her just below her eye. Blood started flowing as she ran up the stairs. Seriously, blood hit every baluster of the white railing. It was the bloodiest battle we had in childhood. She got the worst of it and never misses an opportunity to remind me!*

Our family lived on Elm Street until I was about six and then we moved to Keenan Street in Rogertown between Warren and Clarendon. Mom and Dad bought me a pair of cowboy boots to celebrate the move!

2

Coming from the rural area of Warren County, my first two schools were three-room buildings: Washington (completely gone now) and Lincoln (overhead door company now) elementary schools. I still maintain friendships with  several of those original 28 students. John Gerarde and I were best friends and confirmed this relationship in 2016 in Texas.

Mrs. Dorrion's first grade class

LAUGH WITH ME — I truly enjoyed summer vacations because in kindergarten I thought that school lasted a year and then I had off a year! In second grade the teacher explained the finer points of the nine-month school calendar and the three-month summer vacation. Summers seemed very short after that.

During the early years in Rogertown, Dad developed a machine shop in our two-stall garage and later put on a cement-block addition. His skills were legendary and within time created a pretty good secondary income while still working at Sylvania. Later, he left Sylvania and went on his own to establish the Allegheny Tool Company.

One benefit of the shop was that he taught me how to operate every machine he had. Later this training would afford me the opportunity to work in machine shops while attending college and seminary.

We had a good size lot. I learned how to drive Dad's 1946 Willys Jeep around the perimeter. I sat on a Sears Roebuck Catalog (remember those 2-3" thick books?) and for extra height at age seven, I folded up an Army blanket. I have video to prove it.

Our lot was big enough for many childhood adventures. It was rural and I regularly shot my Sheridan pellet gun at stationary and "moving" targets! I still have it. Later, I wrote an article about it. *(see Appendix, Article 2, Rifles, Respect & Reward).*

I had my first motorcycle at age 13. It was a 1948 Harley-Davidson 125. To test mileage, I once ran it dry and added one quart of gas, noted odometer, then rode around the lot and ran it dry again! It managed 17 miles which equaled 68 MPG. Because of the noise I was **not** my neighbor's favorite kid.

Beaty Junior and Warren Area High School class numbers were swelling with that which is now known as the Baby Boomer generation. The term is used to identify a massive increase in births following World War II.

I was fortunate to attend the newly constructed Warren High as the first class to complete all three grades (10-11-12) in the facility. As a side note, my sister attended the very old original high school and graduated in 1958. She attended an Ivy League High School… because the ivy grew on the inside walls!

Fall has always been my favorite season of the year with the beautiful foliage and color changes. Being from Pennsylvania of course, hunting with Dad consumed my thinking and time.

In October 1962, however, my parent's divorce shattered my life.

As I look back on those high school years I remember the heartache and struggles I had in school. During my sophomore year (1962-1963) I asked God many questions without hearing an answer from heaven.

Little did I know, however, that the Lord was simultaneously initiating awesome plans for my future and preparing one special man plus many more men and women over the next several decades to alter the course of my life for eternity.

An early disclaimer, not one person (especially me) mentioned in this memoir was or is perfect. Only by the grace of God do we have personal significance in life and the legacy we establish for those we influence!

My serious high school picture. For the record, I did letter in one sport. Remember, I am from Pennsylvania where we cling to our God and our Guns! I lettered on the Rifle Team.

5

Beaty Junior High School

Warren Area High School

The Dragon — WAHS Mascot

BETHANY BAPTIST CAMP
JULY 15-20, 1963

Mom and Helen Danielson were good friends. Mom's cousin had married Helen's oldest daughter. They shared many lunches together in local restaurants.

Mom & Helen Danielson
Author's son Mark

After the divorce, Mom worked in the cafeteria at Irvinedale Elementary in Warren with Helen who had been the assistant cook some years at Bethany Baptist Camp and knew that the head cook was not returning in summer 1963.

Helen suggested to the camp board that Mom was certainly competent to supervise the camp food services and might be interested. School cafeteria income was on a nine-month basis so a summer salary would be very helpful.

Sometime in the spring of 1963, a local pastor stopped by our

home to officially interview Mom for the cooking position at Bethany.

He certainly recommended Mom for employment at Bethany. She accepted with one condition: that the camp board would also hire me for something, anything! And they did hire me because they desperately needed a cook! So, I worked that summer, and the next, and the next,

7

and the next as the dishwasher and as a lawn care specialist (1963-1966). *(see Appendix, Article 1, Going Home from the Hospital).*

LAUGH WITH ME — One year Mom baked a lemon meringue pie that was like rubber, definitely not eatable so she put it out on the picnic table for the birds. Dad said that was the first year he could remember that the robins did not fly south… they could not get off the table!

The first week of camp (junior boys) I heard staff praying. This was new for me. I never had heard a group of people praying for the "salvation" of campers or anyone before!

I do not remember the Bible teacher but the missionary was Reverend Terry Armstrong. Although impressed with their special relationship with God, I did not understand the preaching of the gospel or that I needed help… I thought I was a pretty good kid.

INFLUENCE #1

REVEREND MERLIN SHULTZ

My second week of camp (junior girls) brought a new Bible teacher, Reverend Merlin Shultz. Although I had many conversations with Reverend Armstrong the first week I hardly spoke to Reverend Shultz the second week. He seemed quiet and reserved.

However, on Thursday night, July 18, 1963, Reverend Shultz's message was from the gospel of John, chapter 3 and verse 16. Although I had John 3:16 memorized I did not understand that the significance of personal faith was more than memorizing the verse. Then the preacher explained that I needed to acknowledge my sin, put myself in that verse, and to trust the Lord personally as my Savior.

That night I must have read the verse 10-20 times.

For God so loved the world that He gave His only begotten Son, that whoever believes in Him should not perish but have everlasting life.

Reverend Shultz told us to read it and make it personal by placing our name in the verse. Then I read it this way.

For God so loved [DOUG] that He gave His only begotten Son, that [if DOUG] believes in Him [DOUG] should not perish but [DOUG will] have everlasting life. (Prior to Army service, I went by my middle name.)

I invite you to enter your name and believe as I did.

When the preacher asked the 100 plus girls and visiting parents to trust Christ… well, I left the service and had a quiet conversation with the Lord on the outside patio. While I sat there I realized that I needed forgiveness and hope for the future. I prayed and accepted Christ as my Savior and asked Him for guidance. That was the beginning of my new life in Christ.

I knew that Reverend Shultz came from somewhere in upstate New York. I have no memory of further conversations with him that week.

In the 1990's, I learned that he was pastoring in Apalachin, New York. I called him and introduced myself as the dishwasher from Bethany Baptist Camp in 1963. We met soon thereafter for dinner and I thanked him for his ministry in my life.

Much later I wrote the following article about Reverend Merlin Shultz.

A 40 Year Old Blessing Blesses Again, 2004

I love a blast from the past. How about you? During the summers of 1963-1966, I was the dish washer at Bethany Baptist Camp. More eternal events happened those summers than we can possibly know this side of glory!

One sure fact: pastors, particularly one preacher, and missionaries greatly impacted me. Reverend Merlin Schultz, pastor of West Genesee Hills Baptist Church in Camillus (NY), was the preacher the week of July 18, 1963 — the night I gave my heart to the Lord.

For Christians this old world is quite small. That same church which generously allowed their pastor to minister at Bethany in 1963 — well, they now have a new young pastor named Reverend Mark Ferry, the son of that dishwasher who was saved at Bethany almost 40 years ago!

Lesson learned? I believe that God blesses churches that allow their pastors to minister outside their local communities. Congregations may never connect the blessings directly as in West Genny's case, but God always honors those who honor Him, including churches.

A few weeks ago Reverend Merlin Schultz visited West Genny. Pastor Mark was able to honor him and thank him for his ministry during the early days at the church, at Bethany, and in the life of one young dishwasher.

Thank you, Reverend Schultz, you have been a blessing, more than once!

INFLUENCE #2

REVEREND ERNEST HOOK
PASTOR, PENNSYLVANIA AVENUE BAPTIST CHURCH

In the spring of 1963, a local pastor stopped by our home to interview my mother for a cooking position at Bethany. Reverend Ernest Hook's visit began our father/son relationship which has had lasting influences and implications.

Pastor Hook, tall and thin, became the second Christ-Like man to influence my life! Ultimately, it was through him that Mom landed at Bethany Baptist Camp. Also, it was her ultimatum that put me at the camp. Soon afterward I entered into my new life in Christ. It is extraordinary how the seeds of God's grace are sown sometimes before we can even grasp His work or comprehend the fruits of His handiwork. The Harvester is at work in our lives outside our awareness and sometimes even when we least expect it.

Mom accepted with that one condition. They desperately needed a cook so I worked that summer, and the next, and the next, and the next as the dishwasher and as a lawn care specialist (1963-1966).

Up to this time in 1963, my parents had faithfully taken me to church but I had no personal relationship with the Lord. I knew him as a historical figure but not as my personal Savior (*see Appendix, Article 3, Memorial Day*).

At Bethany, during those four summers, I became friends with numerous pastors, missionaries, Bible college administrators, and seminary professors. Each contributed to my Biblical and spiritual development.

Thereafter, Mom and I began to attend Pennsylvania Avenue Baptist Church (Warren, PA) where Reverend Hook was the pastor. Pastor Hook meant far more to me than most ever experience with a pastor!

Pastor Hook was there for me during the three years I did not see my father. He took me hunting and to all tristate church youth rallies (Ohio, Pennsylvania, New York). He invited me to check out the first Ford Mustang to hit Warren in 1964. He enjoyed cars!

Pastor Hook thoroughly taught me the Bible but more importantly he demonstrated both a kind heart and hand. I can still remember his gentle voice and his crippled but gentle hand on my shoulder as he provided sound guidance to this teenager. Pastor and Mrs. Hook had three children: Margaret, Phil, and Paul. All were college or seminary professors during their lifetimes: Phil at Philadelphia Bible College (now Cairn University), Wheaton College, and Dallas Theological Seminary, Paul at Southern Methodist University, and Margaret at Cedarville College (now Cedarville University).

As a new Christian, Pastor Hook was my first pastor. He systematically taught me the Scriptures verse by verse. By actions and attitudes he taught me kindness and Godliness. Pastor was the personification of Christlikeness. One lady in our church said of him, "Pastor Hook is the most Christ-like man I have ever met." I agreed then and still do.

Pastor Hook baptized me in 1964 in Immanuel Baptist Church in Starbrick, Pennsylvania. We just used the facility for the day.

During my last two years of high school, Pastor Hook provided the stability I needed. He was there for me.

I significantly resembled Phil. Our pictures on the piano demonstrated our similar good looks! Pastor and I were together so often that some of my friends thought he was my father. Those who knew him thought that I was his son. Those days were precious.

Dr. Phil Hook   Dr. Allen Ferry

Perhaps I should mention that Pennsylvania Baptist Church met in a storefront. Certainly not clamorous, actually quite barren of stained glass windows or other "religious" items. What this church had however was a godly pastor, solid Bible teaching and preaching. I learned two major principles from this church: first, the primacy of Bible preaching and teaching. Second, the significance of a godly and caring pastor.

Thank you, Pastor Hook for all you provided this teenager in way of Biblical instruction and fatherly example. You are not forgotten.

THINK WITH ME — How important and influential are mentors, role-models, and Godly parents on young men and women on the cusp of adulthood.

Looking back, I can see now the healing salve of God's grace was there all along even when I could not see it… taking care of my basic needs, putting important male figures in my life when I needed them the most, and eventually reconciling the wounds of divorce which, in retrospect, came with unspeakable pain.

I was obviously shaped by Paster Hook's influence on my life. See this in later writings.(see Appendix, article 4, My Father and Friend.)

HIGH SCHOOL friends were important to me. With the advent of FaceBook I have regular communication now with several classmates. I visited with Evan Wolfe and John Gerarde on a trip to Texas. Several times I have had lunch with classmates when I was in Warren. Recently back home hunting deer, I saw Terry and Jeannie Jackson in Arby's and had lunch together.

COLLEGE CHOICES became a significant part of many conversations with Pastor Hook and other pastors I knew from Bethany Baptist Camp.

Sensing a call to ministry but because I was quite young in the Lord, Dr. L. Duane Brown recommended that I needed a solid Bible college to ground me in the Word of God. He recommended Baptist Bible Seminary (BBS) in Johnson City, New York.

Although I did also apply to one other college, I used a pragmatic decision process to make my choice: I would attend the first college which accepted me! Remember, my sophomore year was pretty bad grade wise!

I heard from BBS and eagerly accepted. About a week later the other college accepted me. Looking back, I believe the Lord was totally in the decision. BBS was a great place to learn God's Word, make lifelong friends, and where I met my future wife!

Mom took me for a BBS campus visit and we met Dr. Wendell Kempton who was an instructor, basketball coach, and administrator. He gave us a campus tour which did not take long! In 1965, BBS was a small school on a small campus. Most courses were taught in the classrooms of First Baptist Church across the street from the BBS administration building. BBS actually started in First Baptist in 1932. BBS purchased additional buildings as student numbers grew.

The visit was brief but Dr. Kempton was thorough in his tour and enthusiasm for BBS. Later, he became my basketball coach during my freshman year. He became a good friend and encourager.

CLARIFICATION OF COLLEGE NAMES

Baptist Bible Seminary became Baptist Bible College which is now Clarks Summit University.

Cedarville College is now Cedarville University.

Grand Rapids Baptist College is now Cornerstone University.

Philadelphia Bible College is now Cairn University.

Practical Bible College is now Davis College.

PART TWO

COLLEGE YEARS

1965-1975

BAPTIST BIBLE SEMINARY, 1965

Dad did take me to college to begin my freshman year. It was not a great trip of conversation but mainly silence. We could not talk because we were both entrenched in our painful memories.

When I graduated from High School I held a 3.0 grade point average (GPA). Sounds pretty good, right? However, today most schools and colleges utilize a four point system. Not back in my 1960's high school! Warren Area High used a five point system. So, look at my 3.0 GPA and realize I only had a "C" average grade coming out of high school.

LAUGH WITH ME — I usually tell people the best two years of my life were spent in tenth grade.

So when starting BBS, I was at the bottom of the academic student body. BBS accepted only students with a minimum of 2.0. I barely made it and look back on that acceptance as the grace of God who knew my new heart and desire to serve Him.

I really did not learn how to study in high school. I was not a great student at BBS, however, I did okay. I was motivated by the expertise and empathy of the professors! I remember them with great fondness: Jack Jacobs, Robert Lightner, Walker Barndollar, Donald Launstein, Thomas A. Thomas, and Wendell Kempton.

LAUGH WITH ME — I can remember the cost of tuition my first year. Seems now as ridiculous but in 1965, BBS charged $19.50 per credit hour. I have included this here as a humorous moment because I must have lived in the "good-old-days."

MOTORCYCLES I have had three new Hondas: this 1966 Super 90 was my first in early college years. Many miles without a helmet gave me very blonde hair!

BASKETBALL, 1965-1966

I did not play basketball in high school. However, BBS was such a small college that I tried out for the Defenders team. I think it was safe to say I was the 13th man on a 13-man team. We had some good times traveling with Dr. Kempton. We all wore white London Fog topcoats like his! We wanted to emulate his character and conduct as a personal evangelist. He did not waste opportunities to witness about his Savior.

One night Dr. Kempton asked me to drive him to Horseheads, NY, where he was speaker for a special meeting. (Seems his drivers license was in jeopardy because of a few too many tickets.)

I'll never forget that service. I sat next to him. As the service progressed, he leaned over and said he thought the Lord was directing him to preach a different message. (Not sure why he felt he needed to tell me.) I thought this was very fascinating that he would make adjustment as the Lord directed him.

As Dr. Kempton gave the invitation, I still can vividly see a man walking down the aisle with crutches! The man was Larry Maxson who had recently returned from Vietnam where he lost his leg to a landmine.

The fall of 1966, I saw Larry and remembered him. I introduced myself and welcomed him to BBS. We became friends for life. He pastored until his retirement a few years ago.

WIFE MATERIAL—THERESA HILL

I was age 17 when I graduated from high school and entered college. I was quite immature but certainly knew that I wanted a wife who was surrendered to serve the Lord.

BBS only had about 400 students but Bible colleges are known as "match-boxes" and places where young ladies receive their "MRS" degrees! It was a good place!

When classes began I noticed one young lady who was in most of my classes. We sat near each other and talked between classes.

The more we visited I learned that on Fridays she would walk to the coffee shop near the high school. It was a hang-out for students. Her favorite question over the years has been, "How can I pray for you?" She just asked, listened, talked, and prayed for them.

This dedication to ministry, not a required ministry, impressed me. Her smile and personality also attracted me. Before long we were dating steadily. We paused a few times but I kept coming back to her focus on ministry — not to mention her good looks!

We also shared a week of ministry at Bethany Baptist Camp. I watched her again with teenagers and her question, "How can I pray for you?" I smile each time I hear her ask it.

Eventually, we made a trip to visit her home and parents. The Hills lived in Lockport, New York. I met Cecil, Lorraine, and Theresa's three brothers: Bill, John, and Paul.

Cecil was a deacon at Calvary Baptist Church where they both served faithfully. Lorraine was, well, very special.

L-R: Theresa, Bill, Cecil, Paul, John, Lorraine

INFLUENCE #3

LORRAINE HILL
MOTHER-IN-LAW

But as for you, speak the things which are proper for sound doctrine: that ... the older women likewise, that they be reverent in behavior, not slanderers, not given to much wine, teachers of good things—that they admonish the young women to love their husbands, to love their children, to be discreet, chaste, homemakers, good, obedient to their own husbands, that the word of God may not be blasphemed. —*Titus 2:1-5*

An important preliminary step in finding a good wife is finding a good mother-in-law. Actually, I learned much about my future wife when I observed Lorraine Hill, Theresa's mother.

Lorraine taught a girls Sunday school class for 40 plus years! She never missed church and was a "mom" to dozens of neglected or otherwise less fortunate young ladies. My wife would always identify herself on the phone by saying, "Hi, Mom, this is Theresa." Initially, I thought this strange until my wife told me that so many girls were calling her that she really was not always sure who was calling her "Mom." Therefore, even her daughter would identify herself so not to confuse her mother!

Lorraine was a serious student of the Word. She rode the gospel bus with Dr. J. Vernon McGee for several decades. She knew her Bible; he taught her well, and she studied diligently.

The commencement speaker for my graduation from Dallas Theological Seminary was Dr. J. Vernon McGee. I scored big points with Lorraine when I arranged a private appointment for her to meet Dr. McGee. To meet face to face with her Bible instructor was a big deal for her.

What I saw in Lorraine I also saw in Theresa. She also has a love for God's Word, His people, and the lost. To this day she loves to minister to hurting young mothers whether strangers she meets at the grocery store or long time friends from Lamoka Camp, former churches or new friends on FaceBook.

Like mother, like daughter! I have been doubly blessed by both Theresa and Lorraine!

1965-1966 PHOTOGRAPHS

INFLUENCE #4

DR. JACK JACOBS

Sensing God's call to ministry, I ultimately decided on Baptist Bible Seminary. Many professors were special but one quickly became my mentor and counselor. Dr. Jacobs had a keen mind, quick smile, and listening ear.

These qualities served him well as a college professor and later as a pastor.

During my first few weeks at BBS, Dr. Jacobs sensed in me a hurting heart. I really do not remember how the subject became a conversation nor how the conversation became a counseling session because he quickly became a friend with sound advice that I needed.

Other than bringing me to BBS, I had not seen Dad since the my parent's divorce in fall of 1962. Jack recommended I return home and talk with my father. I followed his advice and the end result was the beginning of a renewed relationship with Dad *(see Appendix, Article 4, My Father and Friend)*.

Dr. Jacobs was one of several Bible/Theology professors at Baptist Bible Seminary. The voices of Wendell Kempton, Robert Lightner, Walker Barndollar, Thomas A. Thomas, are now silent but not forgotten. Recently, I communicated with Dr. Donald Launstein, another great professor, who now lives in Canada where he continues to minister in his nursing home.

Dr. Jacobs was by far my favorite professor. Simply speaking, we clicked with one another.

First, it was his counsel regarding my father. Second, in the fall of 1966, a required extensive physical examination for employment at International Business Machines (IBM) revealed a suspicious "mole" on my chest wall that the IBM physician did not like.

That physician recommended a local dermatological surgeon who removed the "mole" at the Wilson Memorial Hospital in Johnson City, New York. About a week later he called me to his office. He told me to sit down. He said the biopsy revealed a malignancy that necessitated further consultation and probably more extensive surgery.

I immediately walked the two blocks from the physician's office to Dr. Jacobs' office. From that visit, time of prayer, and encouragement, Dr. Jacobs became far more than a great Bible/theology professor, he became my close friend. (I did survive, more later.)

Dr. Jack Jacobs & Son Roger

Our friendship deepened when we worked closely together on the 1968 college yearbook *The Tower*. I immortalized Dr. Jacobs in that book by using a picture of him on my 1966 Honda Super 90. He was that special and the bike was my pride and joy in college!

Also, I did pick up his preaching mannerisms and expressions, none very original but clearly by his influence!

Thank you, Dr. Jacobs, for all you provided for this young student in way of Biblical instruction and godly example. You are not forgotten.

MALIGNANCY

After my visit with Dr. Jacobs, I called Mom and Dad. Dr. Jacobs also arranged for a ride with Dr. William Hopewell to Kane, Pennsylvania, where Dad met me. Dr. Hopewell had a ministry somewhere farther west in the state.

The following day I met with Dad's physician who recommended Dr. William Hall, a cancer specialist in Jamestown, New York. After an extensive exam, Dr. Hall made the following statement: "Considering the malignant matter already removed, the swollen lymph nodes under your arm, and more moles on your shoulder… I believe that without a radical mastectomy you have about a 15% chance of survival."

As you can expect, Dad did not take that prognosis very well nor did Mom when she learned the information later in the day.

We made the decision to go forward with the surgery. It was scheduled for Monday, November 14th. Dr. Hall did the surgery and I returned to his office to have the stitches removed on Friday, the 25th. (I have the dates memorized because the following Monday, the 28th was the first day of deer season in 1966!)

Dr. Hall was very happy to report that additional malignant matter was not found. He said, "I believe your odds have reversed to now you have a 85% chance of recovery!" Mom and Dad were quite relieved.

Less than 2% of those who have this surgery are men; 98% are women! Why did the Lord allow this? That experience with cancer and the radical mastectomy have given me a lifetime of testimony and platform for ministry with those with cancer or who have had the same surgery.

FAMILY MATERIAL—THERESA HILL

In the summer of 1967, with her father's approval, I presented an engagement ring to Theresa and asked the big question to which she answered "yes."

At that time I was working as a salesman for Baptist Life Association which is a fraternal life insurance company. That year they had a contest for the full-time and part-time employees. I worked very hard the that school year and won first place in the part-time employee division. The prize was an all expense trip to Mackinaw Island in upper Michigan.

MARRIAGE & HONEYMOON

We strategically planned our wedding and honeymoon to coincide with the trip. Calvary Baptist Church was sight of the wedding on August 24, 1968, in Lockport, New York. It was a short ride to Niagara Falls where we had dinner. From there we travelled to Detroit for a couple days and then to Mackinaw Island for several more days!

It was a fantastic trip until returning to Clarks Summit, Theresa developed pneumonia and entered a hospital in Scranton. While a patient she developed phlebitis. Fortunately, she was in the hospital and the physicians were able to treat the phlebitis.

Theresa and I rented a mobile home for a while and then a nice apartment in Factoryville. During that time Theresa worked in the cafeteria at Keystone Junior College.

After the honeymoon, I initially worked at MacDonalds in Scranton and later at Eynon Drug in Sugerman's plaza. Each employment provided income for Theresa and me to survive while in college.

However, a few times...we daily ate toasted cheese sandwiches with tomato soup!

SOUTHWESTERN BOOKS

In 1970, without finishing my degree, Theresa and I left BBS. I had signed up for a selling position with Southwestern. I drove to Nashville for a week of training and then drove my 1967 VW "beetle" to Los Angeles. Theresa flew to LA and joined me. We had a small apartment and enjoyed being together in sunny California.

Mid-summer, the mail brought a letter from Mr. McGrew, the BBS registrar, telling me to not return until I could be more focused. Grades had slipped significantly. I needed the wake-up!

I did pretty well selling but the most valuable lesson I learned that summer was how to knock on doors and meet people where they lived. I credit that summer with my easiness at visiting with people of all walks of life in my future ministries.

LOCKPORT

In 1970, when Theresa and I returned east we lived in Lockport near her parents. I continued to sell for Southwestern and did pretty well until the snow started falling! Later, I was hired at a local machine shop where I worked until the following summer.

MARK ERNEST FERRY, JANUARY 9, 1971

While living in Lockport, Theresa gave birth to Mark, our first child. He was born in the Newfane Hospital. He became a great blessing to us and nearby grandparents, their first grandchild.

GRANDVILLE, MICHIGAN

In 1971, Baptist Life offered me an opportunity to represent them in the Grand Rapids area. We made the decision to move and perhaps finish college at the Grand Rapids Baptist College.

I continued to sell life insurance for a few months but eventually went to work at Blackmer Pump, a division of Dover Corporation.

When I interviewed for the machine shop position, the foreman gave me a tour of the plant. At one machine I noticed a petroleum pump that I had significant familiarity. It was one of the pumps I repaired when I was a young boy in Dad's machine shop *(see Appendix, Article 2, Rifles, Respect & Reward)*.

PORT SHELDON APARTMENT

I really enjoyed our apartment in Grandville, especially because it had a small stream ten yards directly just off our back door and patio! I loved the fall when spawning Salmon were cruising upstream!

Not having a rod and reel for such 20-30 pound monsters, I did what any eager angler would do... I put 20 pound test line on my Shakespeare 1775 reel and had at it. Of course the first hooked fish took me upstream and stripped the gears in my reel. I was very sad because I had bought that reel in Warren when I was eight-years-old. I still have the pole but the reel was ruined.

While fishing one day, a man came by and started a conversation. He said he also lived in the apartments. One thing led to another... then the Reverend Bill Commons introduced himself as a missionary on furlough from Hong Kong. That introduction began a life-long friendship.

At that time I was not exactly living the life the Lord had for me. I was discouraged about my departure from BBS. I shared this with Bill and he began regularly praying with me.

One evening, Reverend Eldon Brock, Theresa's former pastor from Lockport, stopped to see us and brought along a friend, Reverend Warren Simmons. The last time I had seen Warren was at his son Dana's memorial service in Clarks Summit.

That unfortunate encounter happened shorty after Theresa and I married in 1968. Our friend Dana became quite sick over Thanksgiving and checked into the local hospital. Bottom line, Dana had Leukemia and died in February of 1969. The memorial service was held in the chapel on the third floor of Jackson Hall. I remember it well, I was a pall bearer who helped carry the casket up three flights of stairs.

Warren was as surprised to see me as I was to see him. His first words were, "I have prayed for you every day since the funeral."

That statement gripped my heart. He had lost his son but he was praying for me!

Eldon just wanted to stop and say hello to Theresa and brought Warren along who did not realize who they were going to visit. I am always amazed with how the Lord arranges these meetings of consequence.

After these events with Bill Commons and Warren Simmons, I connected with Larry Bos, the admissions director at Grand Rapids Baptist College. We determined the required courses for graduation. I left BBS with a GPA under "C" level and a student bill. Because of this, BBS would not release a transcript without the bill being paid. (Ultimately, I paid it.)

GRAND RAPIDS BAPTIST COLLEGE

With Larry's assistance I got back into college. I needed a minimum of 30 hours to complete a Bachelor of Religious Education (BRE) degree. Ultimately, I did transfer over 100 hours from BBS. A blessing was that colleges do not transfer GPA, they transfer credits! So, my sub-C-level GPA disappeared. Also, GRBS, following state guidelines, required a student to have a minimum of 30 hours to graduate.

It took three semesters but I finished and graduated in May of 1973, with a 3.38 GPA on a four-point system!

BLACKMER PUMP/DIVISION OF DOVER CORPORATION

I began working in the Blackmer machine shop the fall of 1971. I'm always amazed at the Lord's provision, shouldn't be, but here is another example.

I was working one evening when another employee asked me if I knew about Blackmer President William Petter's new educational benefit? I did not but quickly applied. His program would reimburse all costs for tuition and books after successful completion demonstrated by an official transcript!

Blackmer Pump paid for the rest of my college education plus books! Interestingly, I believe I was the only employee who completed a degree with this assistance. And further, Mr. Petter ended the program that same year I graduated; designed and timed just for me.

Remember the old encouragement, "Where God guides, He provides." I was shocked but thankful for the Lord using Mr. Petter's educational program to put me through college.

JULAINE MARIE, MAY 18, 1973

I remember the morning Theresa announced that it was time! Off we went to the Butterworth Hospital for the delivery of our daughter (we did not know beforehand).

Julaine had curly, red hair. Theresa said through tears of joy with a big smile, "I have my girl!" We were both thrilled. She continues to bless us.

I came home from the hospital to pick up some additional items for Theresa. While I was putting items in a suitcase I answered a phone call. It was the Human Resource Director from Blackmer asking me to come in early to talk about a promotion. I did and I was. I left the machine shop and became a supervisor in the foundry department. I learned many valuable lessons in supervision and management.

IMPORTANT CONTRAST

Much later in the pastorate I realized a distinction in ministry. In industry the goal is "to get the work done by the people." In ministry the goal is "to get the people done through the work." Ministry is by the people, to the people, and for the people. People develop best when ministering unto others.

GRAND RAPIDS BAPTIST THEOLOGICAL SEMINARY

After college it seemed wise to start seminary while in Grand Rapids. I began in the fall of 1973 and continued to the spring of 1975. I really enjoyed my studies having learned how to study through the process of trial and error. *(see Appendix, Article 5, The Key to College Success)*

Three professors were special for specific reasons.

DR. RONALD CHADWICK made a comment in one class that really made me think. He said, "Look out the window and see that very old vehicle?" He continued, "My wife and I could drive a newer car but we have decided we would rather have our children receive a Christian Education." Dr. Chadwick's one statement made me realize his values were tangible: a new car or Christian Education for his children? He made the right investment.

DR. ANTHONY FORTOSIS taught various Christian School administration courses. I remember one particular emphasis was that an administrator must be a pastor-shepherd of his staff. He was gracious and taught us that kindness must be a virtue of every Christian School administrator.

DR. N.A. WIENS assigned his baptist polity students to write a paper to explain the three offices of pastor, bishop, and elder. This project confirmed the Lord's direction in my life of ministry.

REVEREND TED ERTLE was the pastor of Grandville Baptist Church. He was certainly a gifted teacher. However, I remember most how he showed both his humanity and divine strength when he faced the tragic death of his wife.

Pastor Ertle's writing skill also was a model of clear exposition and practical clarification of doctrine truth and error.

INFLUENCE #5

WILLARD "BILL" & MARIE DOREN

When Theresa and I moved to Grandville, Michigan, we immediately looked for a local church near our apartment. We settled into church life at Grandville Baptist Church which became our home for the next four years.

Some of our fondest memories were created in the homes of Grandville members.

Willard "Bill" and Marie Doren became adopted "Grandparents" to our young son, Mark and later to our daughter Julaine. Bill and I met at church but I also saw him regularly at Grand Rapids Baptist Bible College.

At the time Dr. Wilbert Welch was the college president and had known Bill for many years. Bill originally operated a local auto repair service. Dr. Welch was an appreciative customer and eventually invited Bill to oversee maintenance of the college facilities and grounds.

I remember observing his orderly daily student maintenance assignments on clipboards in neat rows on his office wall. I followed his example in several future chaplaincy ministries.

Bill's most significant influence on my life, however, without doubt was his demonstration of graciousness toward his wife, children, other church members, students and me. It was easy to adopt him as a "father" figure during my college years in Grandville.

After college, I stayed at the Doren's home while taking a graduate course at Grand Rapids Baptist Seminary. I did enjoy the class work but again, the greatest influence during those days was that of two godly people having devotions at the breakfast table.

Bill had very special way of making sure I was up and going! He would stand at the bottom of the stairs and call out, "Daylight in the swamp, Son. Daylight in the swamp."

When the call came announcing Bill's home-going, I knew I would never hear his voice calling me again for breakfast. Our loss was heaven's gain.

However, although his voice may be silenced, his reflection of grace has not diminished. The lessons learned from Bill have been multiplied in my life and ministries.

GROWING CHILDREN

INFLUENCE #6

KENNETH & ELEANOR BOS

I first met Ken and Eleanor Bos in 1972, when I became a student at Grand Rapids Baptist College and attended Grandville Baptist Church. We were impressed with Ken and Eleanor when we learned that they had served as dorm parents for missionary children in the Ivory Coast and had recently returned. They looked a little thin and Tim actually looked like a poster child for Ethiopia malnutrition. I digress!

Ken and Eleanor's home was nearby and often became "grandparents" for our two children when we needed assistance! We trusted them completely.

Ken was an excellent Sunday School teacher at Grandville Baptist. Theresa and I attended his class for several quarters.

Ken was an exceptional teacher. I can still see him carrying his big "cardboard tube" holding drafting paper covered with large notes for illustrations to aid our learning. Obviously he had studied extensively and came prepared to share his findings.

When I took my first pastorate, Ken and Eleanor bought me a nice overhead projector which served me well through three decades of ministry.

We left Grandville over forty years ago but my appreciation for this man of God, faithful servant, awesome teacher, and lasting friend has not lessened.

Ken's reflection of God's grace became a model for my life and ministry.

Thank you, Ken, for impacting my life! We'll meet again.

PART THREE

NEW ENGLAND CHURCHES

1975-1981

Dr. Howard Bixby

I first met Dr. Bixby in 1972, in the parking lot of Calvary Baptist Church in Grand Rapids. I was taking photographs of variously colored objects for a fine arts photography assignment. I was focusing on the Calvary's yellow school buses.

Dr. Bixby suddenly appeared with significant anger in his voice and mannerisms, he asked, "What are you doing?" I explained and he calmed down. Seems others had been plagiarizing his writings and presentations for profit. We became friends that day.

When I was working on my seminary studies I was laid off from Blackmer Pump. I did apply at other machine shops but no one was hiring. Unemployment services mentioned with my education I could be looking for a church.

So, I began looking at churches even though I had not finished my masters degree. When Dr. Bixby called and asked if I might be interested in speaking at his home church in Vermont, I agreed. He and I made the arrangements to visit his church.

East Wallingford & Mt. Holly Baptist Churches Vermont, 1975-1977

Actually three churches were looking to share one pastor and the expenses. Theresa and I drove to Vermont. I spoke in two of the churches: Mt. Holly and East Wallingford. The third church backed out of the three-way option just before we arrived.

E. Wallingford Baptist Church

The two churches extended a call to us to become their pastor and family.

(I have to admit we drove out of Grand Rapids with tears in our eyes because we had come to love our friends at Grandville Baptist Church.)

The two churches were geographically only three miles apart but of two different natures which separated them spiritually.

East Wallingford Baptist Church had a revival some years earlier (1957-59) under the ministry of Paul Bubar, a Word of Life evangelist.

Dr. Bixby writes, "The evangelist who God used in my life to call me into the Gospel Ministry was Paul Bubar. He was a single young man only out of Bible college about one year. East Wallingford Baptist Church was the first evangelistic meetings of his career. As a 17 year old, I organized and led a door-to-door canvasing effort on a Sunday afternoon to invite people to Paul's meetings. It was the first one that the church ever had. The church meetings were packed with town people trying to figure out what this strange thing was that was happening to people at the church." Whole families came to know the Lord. Lives were changed.

Ultimately, Howard went off to Philadelphia Bible College (now Cairn University) and eventually Dallas Theological Seminary.

LAUGH WITH ME — The first Sunday in East Wallingford Church, I announced that we would have prayer meeting in the parsonage on Wednesday evening. A dozen or more people showed up and we had a good time of prayer and fellowship. As people prepared to leave, a deacon asked if we were going to continue having prayer meeting on Wednesdays? I responded, "Why do you ask?" He said, "Well, Pastor, we normally have prayer meeting on Thursday nights."

Mt. Holly Baptist Church had a few good people but most were without a saving understanding of the gospel. In an attempt to bring the two churches together for fellowship, I encouraged alternating evening services monthly between their two facilities. Folks from East Wallingford would travel to Mt. Holly but with a couple exceptions, the Mt. Holly folks would not travel to East Wallingford.

Ultimately, I could not continue as pastor of Mt. Holly. I was sad but the members of East Wallingford were supportive. I picked up supplemental income at a department store in Rutland.

Our EW parsonage was large and inviting. We had youth gatherings and many adults shared meals with us. Theresa became the unofficial "youth director" working with the dozen or so teenagers attending.

LAUGH WITH ME — *Before we left Grand Rapids, we bought a very nice 1964 Dodge Dart from another seminary student who was from California so the Dart was very clean. Arriving in rural Vermont we enjoyed the scenic travel from East Wallingford into Rutland to shop. Theresa made one trip we will never forget. Seems the road crew was giving the highway a new topping of oil, black oil, sticky black oil. Theresa crested a hill and drove for several hundred yards on the fresh oil before she could stop! There were no warning signs nor flagmen! It took several hours to remove the liquid blacktop from the Dart. However, the good news… that Dart never rusted out.*

Our family, 1975   44

BERKSHIRE HILLS BAPTIST CHURCH (BHBC) MASSACHUSETTS, 1977-1981

Daniel Pascucci, long time friend and best man at our wedding, recommended us to Berkshire Hills Baptist, his home church in Lee, Massachusetts.

I remember the call came and we were quite excited to begin this ministry on the west end of the "Bay State" two hours from Boston, one hour from Albany.

We made the move in February of 1977. During packing I pricked my finger with a push pin. (see reflection at end of this section.) I thought very little about it during the rest of that Saturday. I was exhausted, so retired early but woke up quite disoriented in the middle of the night. I waited until about 6:00 a.m. before I called Aldo Pascucci, Daniel's father and deacon. He came and took me to the local clinic. Seems my pricked finger sent an infection into my lymph system and the infection had gone septic!

So, I missed my first Sunday in the pulpit and was out of commission for three days during which time the antibiotics worked. This was the first of many such infections.

Theresa and I enjoyed the people of BHBC. We had a nice parsonage and garden. The view of the Berkshire Mountains was breathtaking!

When we were a pastoral candidate, I informed the deacons that Dad and I had submitted applications for an Elk Hunt in Wyoming. The permits were by drawing and if we were so

fortunate to be picked...
I would be taking time
off to hunt with Dad.
Our names were drawn
and we did the two-week
hunt that October. Dad
and I were both
successful.

To celebrate, Theresa
prepared an Elk steak dinner for the men of the church. We
consumed almost 30 pounds of steak; it was a great dinner.

Lee Christian Academy (LCA) began in 1979. Theresa taught
preschool (ages four & five) the first year and Michele Pascucci
joined her for the second year. LCA served families for twenty
years.

Michele & Theresa

During our time at BHBC, we divided the original lot and sold
the first parsonage on Marble Street. We were blessed to buy the
adjacent house and lot on Pleasant Street and doubled the
church property. Ultimately, we left BHBC debt free.

LAUGH WITH ME — Remember the Dodge Dart? We sold it when we were in Lee. One night a few years later, I was driving home and coming through East Stockbridge I spotted the Dart. I followed the vehicle and when it stopped I approached the young driver. I smiled and told her that it was good to see the Dart again because I was a previous owner. She quickly denied that possibility. She said the car salesman had told her an old couple owned it and did not drive it in the winter. I assured her I was the previous owner when I pointed out the sticker on the back. Theresa bought the sticker in Grandville. It said, "Don't laugh—It's Paid For."

CHURCH PHOTOGRAPH

Because of the slope in front of the church facility, it was difficult to capture a good picture with roofline. The farther away and down the driveway… the less roofline.

So, I climbed a telephone pole with my camera and took this view of the facility which was later line-drawn.

Where there is a will… there is a way!

Reflection — I experienced periods of adversity throughout my life. Things never unfold perfectly. The divorce, the cancer, spotty school performance, becoming septic at such a pivotal time of change. However, God's grace was alive in me and my family's life. God often writes with crooked lines. Grace is perfect even if our lives or events aren't. At pivotal times in my life, I got to where God had planned for me all along… my family, ministry, work in the military and in prisons. However, my path was anything but straight.

See the connection between God's grace and setbacks? I never read too much into my setbacks and have always trusted that being faithful… then God would lead me to who and what I was supposed to become in life. Indeed this is exactly what happened. (see Appendix, Article 12, Blessing on a Bicycle.)

INFLUENCE #7

ALDO PASCUCCI

In 1977, Theresa, Mark, Julaine and I arrived in Lee, Massachusetts when I accepted the call to Berkshire Hills Baptist Church. The church facility set in the beautiful Berkshire Mountains of western Massachusetts. Not far away in Stockbridge was the Norman Rockwell studio and museum. A favorite tourist destination for visiting friends and family.

I was the third pastor of BHBC. I followed Walter Douglass who followed Clarence Kennedy. However, the stabilizing force for decades and I mean "tour de force" (French, literally 'feat of strength') was Aldo Pascucci, a World War II veteran.

Aldo participated in the invasion of Normandy, The Battle of the Bulge and was awarded one Silver and a Bronze Star for six war campaigns. While serving in France, he met Jeannine Lomprez, the love of his life whom he married in France on March 3, 1946.

Returning home with his bride he came to know the Lord as his Savior, became a member of Berkshire Hills and ultimately a deacon who served for many years.

Eulogy — 2014

Memory #1: Although it was 46 years ago, I have never forgotten the fact that the diamond ring that my wife Theresa wears... well, Aldo got it and Dan delivered it. However, I did pay for it!

48

Memory #2:   Fast forward to 1977, I finally met Aldo when I came to preach at Berkshire Hills Baptist Church. His features were striking, his convictions were convincing, and I knew immediately that we were initiating a life-long friendship.

Memory #3:   Aldo demonstrated faithfulness to his family, his church, his community, and me. If the doors were open... Aldo was in church... which always encouraged me. At church and in his home, we prayed together, wept together, and laughed together!

Memory #4:   During my last three visits I witnessed the aging Aldo still actively working to help veterans! During one visit he made sure I left with three very nice shirts; I wore one this past Sunday and thought about him throughout the day.

Memory #5:   Repeatedly, Aldo and I weathered spiritual storms, personal heartache, and yet... many moments of extreme joy.

Knowing Aldo enriched my life. His military service significantly impacted my life--I speak English not German! His friendship encouraged my life. His testimony blessed my life!

Aldo is now home with the Lord he loved and served.

Until we meet again... enjoy your reward, my friend.

COLONEL RUSS MITCHELL retired from the USAF, moved to Lee, and became a farmer. Russ was a quiet man but with significant spiritual depth. Conversations with Russ were always pleasant and informative.

One such conversation became the illustration for the following devotional.

POSSESSIONS & PRIORITIES.

Proverbs 3:9-10
Honor the Lord with your possessions,
*   And with the first-fruits of all your increase;*
So your barns will be filled with plenty,
*   And your vats will overflow with new wine.*

Character is like a fruit-bearing tree. We recognize a tree by the fruit it produces. Godly men honor God by practicing the principle of stewardship. God provides through work and wages; literally the process of planting and harvest. What God provides we possess as stewards for a period of time.

Stewards are responsible for land, wealth, and possessions of another. God evaluates our stewardship by how we handle, invest, and manage His assets that for a period of time are in our possession.

A godly farmer once corrected me when I described his farm as his land. "No, Pastor, I don't own the land, I am just the current steward. This is God's land I just have the privilege to take care of it for a few years!"

How we conduct ourselves as stewards speaks volumes about our respect for God. Do we honor or dishonor Him? He knows and grants more to those who He deems worthy.

If we honor the Lord with our possessions the implication is that He will entrust us with more. However, do not confuse wealth with God's blessing.

How we manage His wealth determines the quality of our stewardship in God's sight.

Jesus said, "Well done, good and faithful servant; you were faithful over a few things, I will make you ruler over many things. Enter into the joy of your lord." (Matthew 25:21)

Servants have a relationship with a master. Stewards are servants who have additional responsibility for what ultimately belongs to the master. A servant becomes a steward when God gives him something to manage.

How are you managing your time, talents, treasure, testimony, and the terra firma?

We come into this world with nothing and we leave with nothing except what is recorded about our stewardship for the Lord.

[Devotionals from Proverbs originally appeared in Allen's "Faith for the Forces" column in the Independent Baptist Voice, 2004-2005.]

DEACON JOHN PERRY drove me the hospital the first Sunday I preached at BHBC. I did not know how to get there. Earlier that day a man called from out-of-state and asked if I would visit his father who was not doing well. John and I found his room and as we entered he said, "With the size of that Bible, I bet my son called you and asked you to see me. I think I need to get saved."

John and I were both amazed as his readiness. We explained the gospel and Mr. Twing accepted Christ as his Savior that afternoon. It was a great way to start our ministry in Lee.

As a historical footnote, I discipled Mr. Twing and was with him when he died. His last words were, "I am ready to go home." He expelled his last breath and passed quietly. His memorial service was the last one I did as pastor of BHBC. His Christian life story was clearly defined; I witnessed both his spiritual birth and physical death.

LAUGH WITH ME — *I have made many preaching bloopers. Classic in Lee was my summary of 1 Corinthians 6:9-11 which reads…*

*"Do you not know that the unrighteous will not inherit the kingdom of God? Do not be deceived. Neither fornicators, nor idolaters, nor adulterers, nor homosexuals, nor sodomites, nor thieves, nor covetous, nor drunkards, nor revilers, nor extortioners will inherit the kingdom of God. And such were some of you. **But** you were washed, **but** you were sanctified, **but** you were justified in the name of the Lord Jesus and by the Spirit of our God."*

My intention was to contrast the past and present lives of the believers noted by the "but" introducing the change of life in Christ.

However, I began by saying here is a list of seriously "wicked livers" who have been changed by Christ. "Wicked livers!" Certainly not what I meant to say.

ELMER & ROSE LANE
A LOOK IN THE REARVIEW MIRROR
EULOGY, FEBRUARY 7, 1997

Some inventions are extremely helpful; take the rearview mirror for example. Although we normally look in the direction we are heading; it is wise to cast a glance backward from time to time to see where we have been and what we have left behind! One rather famous preacher sums up leaving his first pastorate in Massachusetts by saying, "Happiness was seeing New England in the rearview mirror!" I cannot agree with his sentiments.

Although I left Lee, Massachusetts, and Berkshire Hills Baptist Church in 1981, I frequently look back and recall some outstanding memories. And all my memories revolve around people: like camping in the beautiful Berkshire Mountains with my son; dating my daughter at the local restaurant; and preaching to some fine folks at the church. Yes, all my memories involve people.

And some people were very, very special. Two such individuals were Elmer and Rose Lane from Great Barrington. They were unique. Visiting this couple was always a delight. I received more than I ever gave to them as their Pastor.

When I think of Elmer and Rose... I remember their faithfulness.

Elmer participated in my ordination by opening the service in prayer. That day he told me that he was slowing down and would not be able to do some of the things the younger men might be able to do to help in the ministry but he could and would pray for me every day that God granted him breath. I felt the strength that God granted because Elmer effectively and daily brought me before the throne of grace. He was faithful in his commitment to pray.

When I accompanied Elmer on the one way trip to Boston, I asked him a serious question as he was waiting for testing. I said, "Elmer, how are you doing, my friend?" He looked at me and replied, "Well, Pastor, physically I'm not doing very well, but spiritually I am doing just fine!"

Those were the last words that Elmer spoke to me. A look in the rearview mirror reminds me that emotional and spiritual stability grows out of the well tended soil of faithfulness. With his eyes and by his firm grip he communicated his answers to my questions for several weeks. Then he was promoted to glory because he was a person of faith and a faithful person.

Rose was Elmer's special lady. He told me about the time he bought a new car without her knowledge and presented her the keys. He also told me how one son brought her flowers taken from a neighbor's yard! He talked frequently about Rose as his faithful lady.

In church Elmer would often choose to sing the Swedish hymn, Thanks to God for My Redeemer. The first line reads like this...

Thanks to God for my Redeemer, Thanks for all Thou dost provide!
Thanks for time now but a mem'ry, Thanks for Jesus by my side!
Thanks for pleasant, cheerful springtime, Thanks for summer, winter, fall!
Thanks for tears by now forgotten, Thanks for peace within my soul!

But his motivation for his choice shows up in the third verse.

*Thanks for **roses** by the wayside, Thanks for thorns their stems contain!*
Thanks for homes and thanks for fireside, Thanks for hope, that sweet refrain!
Thank for joy and thanks for sorrow, Thanks for heav'nly peace with Thee!
Thanks for hope in the tomorrow, Thanks thru' all eternity!

As we would sing, Elmer would smile and give a glance toward his lady and communicate his love for her once more.

Probably no other act so clearly demonstrates Christ-like love than self sacrifice. A request from a dying neighbor to look after his wife greatly impacted Elmer and Rose's lives. For as long as I knew them, Elmer and Rose cared for Edith, a woman with a "difficult to live with" personality. I think, however, of the words of Jesus, "Greater love has no one than this, than to lay down one's life for his friends." (John 15:13) And lay down their lives they did. When I questioned their tenacity of resolve in the matter, they answered, We gave our friend our word. And Rose continued to care for Edith after Elmer's death. Why? Because she was faithful to Elmer's word.

Faithfulness ran deep in the lives of Elmer and Rose.

Today we gather to remember and honor the lady we all loved. Why do I write and stir our emotions. Because Elmer and Rose Lane left a good mark on a young preacher with a young family. The preacher isn't young any more, but the lesson and memories are still valuable. Faithfulness is a lost character quality at the end of this 20th century. To have it modeled in such sterling quality by the lives of Elmer and Rose — well, God knew I needed to learn something of the cost and value of faithfulness early in my ministry.

Dear family and friends, life is as you view it. Either you consider each day spent and gone or you think of it as invested and eventually bringing a return. It is said that a pastor's retirement benefits are out of this world! This is actually true for all who walk through this life holding Christian values. Investments here... have eternal reward.

Elmer and Rose knew the living Lord Jesus as personal Savior. Thus I assure you that Elmer and his lady have been reunited once more in the glory of heaven.

Elmer left Rose, his special lady, just 18 years ago this month. They celebrated 50 years of marriage while I was their Pastor. I remember the occasion. Family and friends gathered to honor their faithfulness to each other. Once again, today, family and friends are gathered to honor Rose Lane... as a faithful person.

The most significant means to honor the memory of Elmer and Rose is to live the way they lived and be the children of their heritage. Let us be faithful so that another generation may someday look into the rearview mirror and have a good memory of us.

DEACON ROLAND BESAW was called the "Junior Deacon" when I arrived because he was younger, single, and had just been elected.

Roland was an eager student and became a special friend. Quite often we would sang together during the evening service. One of our favorites was by Lanny Wolfe:

Whatever It Takes

There's a voice calling me, from an old rugged tree
And He whispers draw closer to me
Leave this world far behind,
There are new heights to climb
And a new place in Me you will find

And whatever it takes, to draw closer to You Lord
That's what I'd be willing to do
And whatever it takes, to be more like you
That's what I'd be willing to do

Take my houses and lands,
Take my dreams and my plans.
I place my who life in Your hands.
And if you call me someday,
To a land far away,
Lord, I'll go and Your will obey.

And whatever it takes to draw closer to You, Lord,
That's what I'll be willing to do.
And whatever it takes for my will to break,
That's what I'll be willing to do.

Ultimately, this was one influence that led me to return to seminary in the summer of 1981. Another influence was hearing Dr. Howard Hendricks speak in Boston the previous winter. Something about his message created an intense desire in my heart to more seriously pursue a study of God's Word. Because most of my college professors were Dallas Seminary graduates I made the choice to move to Dallas.

Moving our family at this time was not as traumatic as later moves.

PART FOUR

DALLAS THEOLOGICAL SEMINARY

1981-1984

DIMES FOR OUR DAUGHTERS
© SEPTEMBER 1996

I can remember when I could buy a bottle of pop for dime and a candy bar was a nickel. Although that was a few years ago and inflation has changed the value of our pocket change, some things still do not cost much. Dimes and quarters can provide a significant transaction far beyond their monetary value.

Back in the late 70's a young lady came to know Christ in our ministry at Berkshire Hills Baptist Church (Lee, MA). Angie was from a single parent home. Her father was a one night situation. The responsibilities of being both mom and dad eventually proved to be too much for Angie's mom. When her mental state broke Angie came to live with our family. Although Angie was in her late teens she was emotionally much younger than others her age. My wife and I had the privilege and challenge of guiding and teaching Angie, a 19 year old, the basics of family privilege and responsibility.

I started a practice with Angie that has become a great blessing. I would give her a dime each time she would leave our home to go out on a date or basically anywhere else. I would follow up the dimes with a statement along the following lines:

"Angie, you are very special to us. I want you to know tonight and every time you go out of our home that I am not far away. You can use this dime to call me from wherever you are. If you don't like what is happening — call me. If your date is not treating you right — call me. If your group's behavior begins to bother you — call me."

"Angie, you don't have to worry about me being upset over having to drive somewhere to get you — call me and I'll come and bring you home. You don't have to worry about a lecture or discipline or anything — just call me. You see, Angie, I love you and want you to know that this dime is a symbol of my commitment to come to your rescue when you need me. You now have someone who will care for you when trouble comes. Our home is your home and we love you. My arms will always be open to comfort and protect you."

Angie lived with us for almost four years. When we moved to Texas to attend Dallas Seminary, Angie moved with us and the dime routine continued.

Eventually a seminarian noticed her, courtship began and marriage was on the horizon. A few days before the wedding she showed me a bag with all the dimes in it that I had given her. She had every one of them.

She summarized her feeling by telling me she always felt secure wherever she went out. She knew I was available to help her if she needed me. She knew I loved her and that I thought that she was important. Each of those dimes was a reminder of my commitment that I was there for her if or when the situation was beyond her control.

Dimes won't buy a bottle of pop anymore; neither will a quarter. Small change in our pocket can, however, with the right association be a treasure to those we love.

I have given — actually more than that — I have invested many dimes and quarters in my kids and teens at church with absolutely no regrets. For the bigger picture they see is an image of our Heavenly Father Who also gives us the same promise, "Call Me when you are in trouble and I will answer. Don't be ashamed, don't hesitate, call Me. You can always count on Me because you are My child."

Security, yes confidences in His love, interest, and guaranteed forgiveness have brought me back over and over again. When we learn the lessons of His Fatherhood it is much easier to model them before our children.

Is being an example of our Heavenly Father's love and assurance of security a rewarding experience? Yes it is. Angie gave her first father's day card to me. I still have it and the others that followed! Yet more precious than the memories is the fact that she and her husband presently serve in Colorado as an associate pastor and family.

The Father in Heaven loves to touch the lives of single parents and the fatherless. His plan includes us. James tells us, "Pure and undefiled religion before God and the Father is this: to visit orphans and widows in their trouble, and to keep oneself unspotted from the world" (James 1:27).

Mark, Julaine, Angie
Theresa, Allen

Mr. & Mrs. Daniel Druyor

61

MOVING TO DALLAS WAS AN ADVENTURE. Packing itself was challenging. The trip was exhausting. That summer of 1981, the heat was so terrible that roads out west actually were buckling. We had to drive carefully through Oklahoma where the roads were the worst.

We bought a nice home in Mesquite without employment because I had a decent downpayment provided by three friends from Grandville Baptist Church. I had already applied for machine shop work and security. Most responded that I was overqualified. I did find work with Purolator Armor for a few months before being hired at Gardner-Denver Corporation in Mesquite.

I thought the machine shop was like being paid to have a hobby. I ran the largest lathe in the shop. It had a 48" swing and 120" bed. One cut could take 45 minutes. We created very large spools for oil drilling rig cables during a booming oil business time.

I worked at Gardner-Denver for about six months before a layoff, during which time I was thankful for the good pay and steady income.

FAST FORWARD to my retirement at age 65. I received a nice letter from Pacific Life requesting verification of my social security number and address. I called the 800 number and confessed that I did not have life insurance with Pacific Life. The very nice lady asked if I worked for Gardner-Denver in Mesquite. I confirmed that I did. She explained that the company had established a retirement plan for me through Pacific Life and would I now like to receive it? That took a nanosecond to respond positively! I did not ask how much. The pleasant surprise came in the mail in a few weeks and the direct deposit has been consistent every month. Six months work, good pay, and a small but lifetime retirement. God is so good.

The Lord also graciously and unexpectedly provided in other ways. *(see Appendix, Article 12, Blessing on a Bicycle)*

DALLAS THEOLOGICAL SEMINARY (DTS), 1981-1984

DTS is considered by many as the premier seminary in the United States. Of course, most graduates definitely hold DTS in high regard. There are many other good seminaries and I did consider Grace Seminary in Indiana but the employment situation in Warsaw was not promising.

I truly enjoyed my studies at DTS. The professors were very much the best of the best in my eyes. I was learning from the men who wrote the books I had studied for years. Such names as Dwight Pentecost, Charles Ryrie, John Walvoord, Howard Hendricks, Stanley Toussaint, and Roy Zuck to mention a few.

I have decided to only mention those who most greatly influenced me and for specific reasons.

INFLUENCE #9

DR. DWIGHT PENTECOST

I always sat in the first row directly in front of Dr. Pentecost. One class vividly demonstrated his understanding and appreciation for eschatology (future events). Seems that a former student had written somewhere that the most unimportant class he had at DTS was eschatology. Well, let me tell you... Dr. Pentecost was alive with indignation and righteous anger. Remember, I am sitting only five or six feet from him.

His 75 minute response was to list reasons for the importance of knowing the future as the Word of God reveals it. The most lasting illustration was the preaching of funerals for believers. He said, "Men, when you preach a funeral, you better know your eschatology. Your hope, your comfort, your salvation, your certainty... all reside in the Word of God and it is all eschatology!"

I may not have quoted him at every memorial service I have conducted but his voice still lingers in my mind and heart.

Thank you, Dr. Pentecost for your faithfulness in reminding this seminary student the great value of eschatology.

DR. ROY ZUCK

Most certainly I worked harder for Dr. Zuck than any other professor. His classroom excellence and comprehensive knowledge motivated my driving desire to emulate him. His truckloads of handouts must have killed whole forests. I still have a file full of his notes. I have used them in my classes — copied and credited to him.

Thank you, Dr. Zuck, for your excellent example of teaching.

INFLUENCE #11

DR. HOWARD HENDRICKS

Probably the most widely known DTS professor, Dr. Hendricks personified excellence in understanding and motivation.

During his introduction and explaining the syllabus for Basic Bible Interpretation, Dr. Hendricks clearly made the content of the syllabus a matter of great importance. His presentation was highly motivational and the result became revival-like in student response. I have never forgotten the importance of telling the destination and then laying out the directions on the map.

Thank you, Dr. Hendricks, for your excellent example of motivation.

INFLUENCE #12

DR. LANIER BURNS

When thinking about the influence of DTS professors, my mind comes back to a Monday morning class after a very sad weekend. Seems a DTS student had a moral failure with another student's spouse. Every class Dr. Burns started with prayer but on this particular day he asked us to pray for those involved; not by name, of course, but to pray for them. In the  midst of his request for prayer, Dr. Burns began to weep over these men and women. I witnessed a brilliant and theologically astute man weeping over the damage of sin. He taught me something by tears that lectures cannot teach. Dr. Burns had both a brilliant mind and sensitive heart.

Thank you, Dr. Burns, for demonstrating compassion and empathy for your students.

Dr. Gene Getz

Although we were members of Maranatha Baptist, for several weeks we attended Fellowship Bible Church in Richardson on Friday evenings. I had fond memories of the Dr. Getz's books I had read and wanted to personally hear him preach.

I admit I do not remember any of his sermons, however, I remember one lesson he taught by example. The service started with one song. Dr. Getz then came to the pulpit, announced that he would preach first, then leave because his son was playing his final high school football game, and he had promised his son that he would be there by half time!

Thanks, Dr. Getz, for the fatherhood lesson so vividly presented.

PART FIVE
NEW YORK CHURCHES

1984-1998

THE VILLAGE BIBLE CHURCH (VBC)
1984-1986

While finishing my final year at
DTS, several churches contacted
me about speaking and
interviewing for their pastoral
positions. Churches in Indiana,
New York, and Pennsylvania were
quite eager for me to answer their
questionnaires.

I may not be the most innovated
individual but I knew I could not
take four to six hours for each one.
When I approached Dr. John
Reed about using the video recording equipment using for
practice preaching, he agreed.

So, I set up the equipment, answered the questions, and taped a
brief devotional. I did this for the last three churches and all
three invited me to visit them.

One church did not quite line up with my positions when I
pressed for more information. One church was close to a great
seminary where I thought my skills would not seem to match
well.

When the final call came we decided to accept the call to the
Village Bible Church in Fonda, New York.

CHALLENGING TIMES

A group of people came together to start Village Bible in 1982.
The first pastor grew attendance by concerts and story-telling.

He had a charismatic and strong personality but lacked in other qualities. When he had moral failure, he left behind his wife and son.

The church had attracted some very fine people, yet who were discontent with previous area churches. I was told that the closest Baptist church had eight pastors in six years! Thus the VBC decided to use "Bible" not "Baptist" in the church name.

Biblical exposition drew many folks to VBC and attendance roughly doubled to over 200 in a few months. We established a Sunday school and utilized a neighboring restaurant space for necessary classrooms.

However, some folks raised issues of concern; some were real, some were perceived but not real. Some dear folks never truly unpacked and talked about leaving.

Ultimately, I resigned because the conflict was becoming very painful for Theresa and our family. Blessings, however, came in the number of folks saved and enduring friendships.

LAUGH WITH ME — I had one preaching blooper at Village Bible that literally stopped the service. I was relating back to Camp Bethany days, how we would demonstrate our final surrender to God at the Friday night campfire service. With all seriousness I said, "We would pick up a "faggot" and throw it into the fire to indicate our surrender!"

From the back of the auditorium I heard Mountain Man Jake call out, "Throw one in for me, too, Pastor!" The service was over.

My term meant a bundle of sticks or twigs bound together as fuel. not the more recent derogatory reference to male homosexuality.

INFLUENCE #14

ROSE GARREN

During the first year in Fonda, a young fellow came to church with his cousin. I always greeted four-year-old Robbie and asked about his family and encouraged him to bring them all.

Within a few weeks, Robbie came with his mother Rose in tow! He brought her to church and she became regular in attendance.

Rose listened and often indicated at the invitation by raised hand her interest and need of a personal relationship with the Lord. However, she told me one Sunday as she was leaving, "Pastor, I still have some questions."

I said, "Well, Rose, stop by the parsonage any afternoon. Theresa and I will do our best to answer your questions."

We set a day and time. When she arrived she produced her notes and questions. I really don't remember the initial ones but I have a clear memory of the last one. Rose asked, "What do you believe about UFOs?"

In all my years, before or since, I have never been asked that question! However, she was serious — so I was. I answered, "Rose, much has been written about UFOs and almost all is based on *speculation*. As a pastor, I deal with *revelation* and the Word of God is concerned about our relationship with Christ. If I have answered your other questions… are you ready to receive Christ as your Savior?"

Rose said, "Yes, I'll get saved next Sunday morning!" To which I encouraged her to pray with us then and confess her salvation the following Sunday. This is what Rose did. I will never forget that weekday afternoon and the UFO question.

Eventually Rose became my church secretary. She was an eager student of the Word and excellent secretary.

Influences come in a variety of forms. Rose influenced me by her sincere search for truth and relationship with the Lord. Her desire was real, her questions came from a thinking mind.

Thank you, Rose, for your friendship, encouragement during difficult days, and yes, your questions!

GROWING INTEREST IN ARMY CHAPLAINCY

My introduction to Captain Dan Szabo was during the first visit that Theresa and I made to VBC. We were having lunch at Tom and Ruth Becker's home. I remember Dan in uniform driving a camouflaged truck stopping to ask me about becoming a chaplain in the Guard.

The idea interested me because Dad served in the Guard and deep down I always thought I would enjoy that ministry environment. But the history of cancer made me ineligible years earlier, however I committed to investigate the possibility.

I did inquire and initiated the process. The National Guard gave preliminary approval.

The four requirements are: First, a recognized bachelors degree; second, be under 40 years of age; third, have a recognized Masters of Divinity or equivalent degree; and fourth, pass the entrance physical.

The more I prayed about the chaplaincy, the more convinced that the Lord was leading in this unique ministry.

However, the educational requirement was for resident course work. I had some hours by extension so I was not qualified... yet.

After thorough research of graduate seminaries offering doctoral degrees, I settled on Trinity Evangelical Divinity School (TEDS) in Deerfield, Illinois. Inerrancy was important to me and accessibility by air was also. TEDS had and still has a great Doctor of Ministry program.

During the coursework timeframe, the new National Guard medical officer decided that my history of cancer and muscle removal were not waiverable. I was quite discouraged to say the least.

I completed the educational residency requirement in July 1987. However, I still had the physical non-waiver issue!

During my last week of classes, as is my habit, I wanted to attend a local church prayer meeting. So, I borrowed a car and visited a small church in Deerfield. I knew of the pastor but did not know him personally. He did a nice presentation on the tabernacle and then he said we would break up to pray.

At that point a man came up to me and asked me to join him. We went downstairs. He asked me if I had any special prayer requests.

I told him that I hoped to became a military chaplain but the National Guard Bureau (NGB) had declined my application.

Then he said, "Well, maybe I can help. I am an active duty Army advisor out here at the local Reserve Center. I worked for the chaplains at my last assignment at Fort Meade. I'll check with them tomorrow and see if they can help." He asked if I had my paperwork with me. I did!

We were strangers less than an hour earlier but the Lord certainly makes His appointments on time.

I sent off the paperwork. The Army Reserve did ask for a new physical examination and statement from an orthopedic surgeon. With that completed, my packet went forward and I was approved.

I immediately called Captain Dan Szabo to give me the oath of office. I raised my right hand and I was officially commissioned on September 29, 1987, eight days before my 40th birthday.

Thank you, Lord, Captain Dan Szabo, and Sergeant Christian! Yes, the Sergeant's name was "Christian." The Lord has a sense of humor.

TRINITY EVANGELICAL DIVINITY SCHOOL
1986-1989

The educational concept of the Doctor of Ministry program is to integrate classroom learning with a clinical or church setting. All classes required local church application. All my study and work assignments were used in the ministry of the Village Bible Church.

I had amazing professors at TEDS. However, one professor and I connected in a most unusual way.

INFLUENCE #15

DR. DAVID LARSEN

I had Dr. David Larsen for a preaching course. His assignment was for his students to develop special ways or methods of preaching.

I came prepared. He came prepared.

Dr. Larsen said he would begin with a first-person narrative. Thus he began, "Good morning, my name is Philemon." Speaking in character he told his story.

When he finished he asked if anyone would like to volunteer. My hand was the first one up!

I began, "Good morning, my name is Onesimus." Dr. Larsen had great difficulty keeping his composure. You see, Philemon and Onesimus are the two primary characters of the Biblical book Philemon. He said this was the first time in his teaching career that a student chose a character which perfectly dovetailed with his. Obviously, I got an "A."

Additionally, Dr. Larsen came from the Swedish Covenant Church denomination. He helped me better understand that the Covenant had a wide variety of evangelical positions. My home church in Warren was not the best… according to his estimate. I agreed.

LEE PUBLICATIONS, 1986-1988

I did quite a bit of banquet speaking in the early days of ministry. While at VBC, we hosted a couples banquet and invited Fred Lee's church to join us.

In the good old days I had a pretty good memory. I would memorize the names of guests as they arrived and use them in the messages. Fred was impressed with what he called, "My party trick!"

Before I resigned from the Village Bible Church, I approached Fred about transitional employment between Village Bible and future ministry. He was kind to open the door and presented an opportunity for me to start a newspaper: *Career & Higher Education News*.

Fred had a knack of starting "penny saver" format papers that provided news and opportunity for advertising sales. His successes included *Hard Hat News* and *Country Folks*.

I worked for Fred from August 1986 to January 1988. I resigned when I reported to Fort Monmouth, New Jersey for chaplaincy basic training. I learned valuable skills at Lee Publications, including print layout and editing. Every employment along my life journey has equipped me for various aspects of future ministry.

US ARMY RESERVE (USAR)
UTICA, NEW YORK, 1987-1989

With Sergeant Christian's help, I was commissioned into the United States Army Reserve (USAR) and began serving with the 331st General Hospital in Utica, New York.

A note of clarification is in order. The USAR is under the sole control of the President. The Army National Guard (ARNG) and Air National Guard (ANG) are under the authority of both the President and the fifty Governors of the individual states. The USAR is never used for local disasters; that would be the National Guard. USAR is comprised of support units like medical, civil affairs, laundry, water handlers, etc.

Another distinction, the USAR train/drill in Reserve Centers, the ARNG train/drill in Armories. The ANG usually share air bases with the active duty United States Air Force (USAF).

My time with the USAR commenced with the commissioning. I began to drill in October 1987. I reported for basic training at Fort Monmouth, New Jersey in January 1988. I was 40 at that point and one of the oldest class members.

CHAPLAIN BASIC OFFICER COURSE (CHOBC)
FORT MONMOUTH, NEW JERSEY
JANUARY-APRIL 1988

I really was looking forward to the physical training at Fort Monmouth. However, I knew I would need to get into shape!

At that time, the Army had three events for physical qualification: push-ups, sit-ups and the two-mile run.

So, I started early to prepare for the anticipated running. Using my vehicle I measured the distance up Hickory Hill Road to the one mile mark; thus up and back equalled two miles. I remember the first morning in October that I ran it. I had to stop eight times in the two-mile distance. Boy, I was out of shape; frankly, I never was in shape!

However, I ran every morning until I was able to complete the two miles under 18:43, the maximum timeframe for age 40. I was ready when I went to Fort Monmouth. To max the run I would need to run the distance under 14:43.

Sit-ups were not a problem and I had a waiver for push-ups because of the radical mastectomy. By the end of the course during the qualifying run I did max the two-mile run in 14:41. My best ever!

Basic training was mostly classroom instruction. I enjoyed the map reading and survival skills training. The most useful classes, however, were Basic Human Interaction (BHI) and Active Writing.

BHI empathized active and responsive listening. I have regularly used the technique since. Active writing discouraged the rampant and excessive use of passive tense. I still carefully avoid passive tense.

The two-phase basic course lasted from January to April of 1988. Some came just for the first phase with the intent of finishing the second phase later. Some came just for the second phase having already finished phase one. Because I was "unemployed" leaving Lee Publications and looking for a pastorate when I returned, I completed both phases. I'm glad I did.

I enjoyed the training and military discipline. I still arrange my clothing with proper spacing between shirt and pant hangers!

I loved the uniforms; no worries about mismatched colors!

LAUGH WITH ME — I did quickly learn the value of sewn-on rank and insignia when I reported to formation one morning without my normal pinned-on type rank. The course manager called me "Private Ferry" the rest of the day! I learned quickly.

I was one of five or six men over age 40 at the school. As I remember it, Chaplain (MAJ) James Buckner, the course manager, did ask if those over 40 had their "over 40 physical?" My roommate, Dan Viveros, and I did have a physical when we were over 40 but the Army has a special physical for "old" people! We did not want to observe training and exercise from the sidelines… so we remained silent. So, Dan and I did all the physical training requirements; the others did not.

In the United States Military cadences sung by marching or running soldiers are often dubbed "Jodys" or "Jody calls." This name "Jody" refers to a recurring civilian character, the soldier's nemeses, who stays home to a perceived life of luxury.

As spring and Easter approached I tried to write something Biblical for the troops to sing. This is what I wrote.

RESURRECTION CADENCE, 1988

Got up this morning at quarter past seven,
      Couldn't stop thinking about going to heaven.
So grabbed my Bible and my wife,
      Headed for the chapel to learn about life!

Members of the choir were singin' a hymn,
      The preacher was preaching about new life in Him.
They were preachin' and singin' about the Lord.
      I sat up straight, I was not bored.

When he talked about sinners, he looked at me.
      He said Jesus loved sinners just like me.
Jesus came to prove God's love is great.
      Without a doubt it is our sin He hates.
Jesus died on the cross my soul to save.
      Just three days later He arose from the grave!

It's Resurrection Sunday -- Good News it brings.
      The preacher is preaching while the choir sings.
It's Resurrection Sunday -- God raises the Son,
      The work of the Spirit in my heart has begun.

I heard the preacher say, "Jesus died for me."
      He went to cross to set me free.
I heard the preacher say, "Jesus lives for me."
      Now I know the difference, the truth I can see.

I can see the cross through the open tomb.
      It is an empty cross that dispels my gloom.
I can see the tomb through the open door.
      It is an empty tomb, death rules no more.
Jesus in in Heaven interceding for me.
      Thus I am forgiven and happy as can be.

Today I became a child of the King.
      I have a new song in my heart to sing.
I'm so glad I grabbed my Bible and my wife.

And went to chapel to learn about life.
Glad I went to chapel and heard the preacher say.
The Savior is in Heaven and He leads the way.

I remember our February "field experience" at Fort Dix included bitter 16 degree temperatures the first night. We were issued individual tents and very thin Vietnam or Korean era sleeping bags! Chaplain Buckner came to the rescue and issued us green "Army blankets" which saved us during several cold nights!

However, I came prepared from New York and brought long underwear. I was cold but okay. Some men from California and other western states stayed all night in the latrine with salamander-type kerosene heating units. The smell was terrible!

CALVARY BAPTIST CHURCH CONNECTION

During our field experience, the mail came. While in my one-man tent, I opened a letter from Reverend Ken Elgena, the alumni director then for Baptist Bible College (now Clarks Summit University). He informed me that he had submitted my name to Calvary Baptist Church in Richland, New York.

I opened my New York map but could not find Richland. I said to myself, "Lord, You do have a sense of humor; You want to humble me!"

A nice church in New Jersey did invite me to speak over Easter weekend. However, the deacons did not have time to meet with me. Eventually, they did extend an invitation to candidate.

I came home at the end of April. My in-laws were there to welcome me. It was good to be home.

When Deacon John Jacobs from Calvary called, I told him I had been home for about 45 minutes and wanted to have uninterrupted time with my family. He agreed to call again and would send pertinent information.

We did talk later and set a Sunday to visit Calvary in May of 1988. John did also send the constitution, annual budget, and a few other documents. When I looked over the budget, I was quite perplexed to see the very low salaries for both a Senior Pastor and a Youth Pastor.

I immediately called John and told him I would keep the speaking engagement but that I could not begin to support my wife and two teenagers on the budgeted amount. Actually, combining the two salaries would be closer to reasonable. I will not state amounts because this was 1988 and Calvary had good intentions.

However, as I told John, the budgeted pastoral salary was seriously out of line for a church the size of Calvary especially when the budget included a youth pastor! John promised he would work on the salary.

It may sound that I am money driven but as a husband and father my first responsibility is to my wife and family. I cannot remember who originally taught me but my grid for decisions must have these priorities: God first, wife and children second, ministry third, and vocation fourth.

I have to put God first in my life, His will, His direction, and His guidance for daily moral decisions. This guidance led me to Bible college and to Theresa.

I have to put Theresa, later Mark and Julaine, before ministry. As Dr. Hendricks has often been quoted, "If it doesn't work at home, don't export it."

Ministry and vocation choices blur somewhat for those choosing ministry as a vocation.

My decision process, however, included the following. I knew that the Lord called me into pastoral ministry: God's call and direction. However, I was responsible for my family before ministry choices.

Let me insert my son's view on this decision process. He created the Sacred Seven for married individuals with spouse and children. Six in the mix with only a spouse. Five when single.

I think this is quite clear and more thoroughly developed than mine.

"Sacred Seven"
"Fab Five"
"Six In The Mix"

#1—God
#2—Mate
#3—Children
#4—Ministry
#5—Job
provides $ for...
#6—Family Ministry
#7—Life Ministry

First Visit to Calvary Baptist Church, May 1988

Our visit to Calvary was a tremendous time with some very dear people. I witnessed Theresa smiling in the midst of the ladies. She was once again in her element. Mark and Julaine were equally welcomed by the youth and leaders. However, Mark was less excited about leaving Fonda where he had done well in track! (More later on Mark.)

Response to preaching was enthusiastic. One young adult professed faith in Christ.

True to his word, John Jacobs did a pastoral salary survey of like-minded churches of approximately same size in the general area. He presented his findings to the deacons and ultimately the budget was adjusted to a livable salary for our family.

After the service, as chairman of the deacons, John asked if we would consider returning to preach again. I was quite encouraged.

However, I was not 100% certain. The church in New Jersey was still interested. I was scheduled for two weeks military training at Fort Drum. Theresa and I needed time to pray for direction.

Later in May I reported to Fort Drum to work with a hospital unit.

I remember Military training exercises involved mass casualties and ministering to the wounded. I had to sign records of all with whom I had conversations. Later, I wrote letters (for the commander) to the families of the deceased. One victim died within minutes after my prayer with him. This situation, albeit a simulation, was a lesson in the finality of life and importance of Army chaplaincy!

While at Fort Drum, Theresa and I talked regularly and came to peace with declining the New Jersey invitation and agreeing to candidate at Calvary.

I remember the telephone booth I used (before cell phones).

First, I called the New Jersey church of over 300 members and expressed appreciation for their interest and invitation but sensed the Lord was leading us to Calvary of less than 100 members. The size was not determinative. Overwhelming warmth of Calvary, quality leadership, and area potential were key factors the Lord used to direct us to candidate.

Second, I called Calvary and accepted their invitation to candidate. We set a date for a week of interaction and fellowship.

That week after the phone call, I dropped into a Wednesday Prayer Meeting and was warmly welcomed. The facility was alive with adults, teens, and children... in Richland—the center of nowhere!

The candidating week was an excellent time of meeting families in their homes! More and more impressed with these wonderful people and the clear purpose they had for their church.

CALVARY BAPTIST CHURCH
1988-1998

The call to pastor Calvary came immediately after their congregational meeting. If I remember correctly, the final vote was 94% of about 50 voting members. My humor was too much for two or three. I told no jokes or humorous illustrations, however, something did make me laugh during a message and that was not acceptable to a few.

FIRST YEAR

The Calvary facility was formerly a Methodist church. The pews had a lacquered finish and very old dusty padded cushions. I remember seeing ladies' dresses stick to the back of pews when the summer-heat basically melted the lacquer. It was sad.

Before my family arrived, I visited all the families of the church. I asked every family, "What three ways spiritually and three ways physically can we improve the church ministry?" Number one physical improvement was to upgrade or replace the seating.

I agreed that a good project would be to replace the pews with individual seating. However, first I did a cost comparison. Wood pews were/are very expensive. Individual setting varied by quality of chairs. I ordered two or three pricing options and had them by the second deacon meeting in Jim and Lois Roberts's apartment where I was still staying.

When we got to "seating" on the agenda — I pointed out that they were sitting on the options! They approved the project and our congregation was sitting on new chairs within the first year.

I remember that we literally had standing room only on Father's Day 1989. Immediately the deacons and I talked about our options.

SECOND YEAR

Within two months we initiated two services and classes between. However, this did not solve the problem of crowded classrooms because a large percentage of those worshipping also wanted to attend classes.

Again, we adjusted and introduced a schedule of simultaneous services and class electives. Service and class times were 9:00 to 10:10 and 10:30 to 11:40. The choir sang at the beginning of each service and then continued in worship or members would then attend the classes of their choice. Folks either chose their elective and then worshiped the other timeframe or the opposite. Of course some just attended the worship service of their choice and did not attend a Bible Class.

We continued this schedule for several years.

STEELHEAD FISHING

Salmon River had great Steelhead fishing. Remember that most of the Lord's first disciples were also fishermen! Just saying!

LAUGH WITH ME — I was discipling a young fellow who liked to fish. One winter morning I picked him up very early and off we went to the Salmon River. I had neoprene wadders but I quickly become numb. My line froze. I could not feel my fingers. I finally said, "We're out of here!" Later in town I checked the bank thermometer. It read, "-4" in green numerals, but I was very blue!

ASSOCIATE PASTOR

Calvary continued to grow and the desire for a "youth pastor" was a high priority. In early 1989, I did a survey of the adults and learned that the average adult ages were 42 for the men and 43 for the ladies. Thus the number of teens was significantly high.

I remember that some wanted a "youth pastor" but some saw no need for an "associate pastor." My thought was that the ministry description would include the youth. However, I wanted the church family to respect the new staff member as a "pastor" but with specific yet different responsibilities from mine.

With deacon agreement, we began a search for an "associate pastor."

Remembering that I had successfully used video to answer questionnaires from churches, I asked Jim Roberts to help create a video to provide an overview of Calvary's ministries. I can still see Jim carrying a huge VHS type recorder on his shoulder as he went throughout the building recording classes and the congregation.

Afterward I added a series of questions on the tape. Ultimately, I sent the video to six or seven potential candidates. Several good men responded. However, one was a standout.

INFLUENCE #16

REVEREND KENNETH YOUNG
1989-1997

I remember Ken's video response clearly demonstrated his love for youth ministry, adult ministry, and certainly people in general.

Ken had good academic credentials but it was his heart that caught our attention. His answers were not only from his educational preparation but from his tender heart. The deacons and I agreed unanimously that the Lord had led us to Ken. So we officially invited him to visit Calvary as a candidate for the "associate pastor" ministry.

Ken's visit initiated our friendship of thirty years (1989-2019)! He is now 60 years old but forever "Young" if you get what I mean.

Ken and Vicki's visit was love at first sight. Immediately they were part of the Calvary family!

LAUGH WITH ME — When Ken applied as a potential Associate Pastor, he mentioned that he knew how to juggle. So when he came to visit, I asked him privately to teach me how to juggle!

I remember his careful instruction and my initial feeble attempts... quickly progressing into a very professional juggling technique.

Ken was absolutely amazed. Surprise: I have been juggling since high school. Got him!

Calvary extended a call to Ken and Vicki to become our first Associate Pastor and wife. They became far more than staff... they became family members. Theresa and I were with them when both daughters were born. I was with Ken all night when Vicki was rushed to the hospital with critical physical complications. We are so thankful she came through that scary night.

All in all, I can say that the eight years Theresa and I shared with Ken and Vicki at Calvary were the best years of our pastoral ministry. Theresa and I still love these two fine servants.

Widows & Orphans

Although the construction in 1997, of the new facility was significant and I have many memories associated with it... the most precious memories always include people.

TARA (NEESE) SHEFFER was not a happy teenager when she came to Calvary with her mom whose pastor had recommended Calvary and me in particular. Lin decided to remove Tara from the bad influences of her previous city school system but Tara was not thrilled with the move to the country.

I remember the silent treatment she gave whenever I attempted to talk with her. When the annual Father and Daughter Banquet provided an excuse to do something special for Tara, with my daughter's permission I wrote this letter for her.

Fathers & Daughters
June 20, 1994

This is a very special night for me, Tara. You have granted me the privilege of sitting or standing beside you in a father and daughter relationship. I am proud to accompany you tonight.

Life sometimes has its fateful turns and unusual circumstances. I remember well the heartache of my broken home without my father. I loved both my mother and my dad and it was hard to accept his absence after the divorce. My situation was turned around about three years later... but your situation may never change.

And if that is the case, then you will have to accept whatever happens. You can rise above your circumstances and live successfully. God will grant you grace and wisdom for every situation. You are already demonstrating fine qualities of maturity. I am very proud of you.

About tonight — many suggestions are going to be offered about how fathers and daughters can be servants together. Each time a reference is made about dads or fathers I want you understand that this evening is not for show but that I want to be by your side every time "Dad" should be there.

Tara, you can call on me...
- *when it is time to learn to drive.*
- *when you are performing a concert.*
- *when you are confused and need a listening ear.*
- *when you need advice about boys.*
- *when you need help with tough decisions.*
- *when you are playing basketball, volleyball, etc.*
- *when you need help with college choices.*
- *when you are treated wrongly and are hurting.*
- *when mom just doesn't understand.*
- *whenever you need me!*

The reality is that I am not perfect (Theresa, Mark & Julaine will attest to this!). So don't look to me to be a perfect example. Remember that the Lord is deeply interested in your life. He should be your ultimate provider of guidance and encouragement. I found His love and interest in me as a result of my parent's divorce. We must remember that He is in control. If you trust Him, He will bring beauty out of ashes. He will quench your thirsting soul with everlasting water. I know — He did for me.

Tonight will be over in a few short hours, but the promise of this letter will outlast any flowers I may have given you tonight. If your dad walks back into your life... I will not be needed. But until he does... I am here. You see, Tara, when I was left without my Dad, the Lord put Pastor Ernest Hook into my life. Perhaps I can in some measure return my debt to him by investing in your life. Let's plan some ways to serve the Lord together!

You are loved, Tara. Enjoy the evening, young lady.

That banquet was followed by attending numerous concerts, basketball games, etc. When promised funds did not arrive for school clothing... I bought them.

Rewards included a growing smile on her face, involvement in youth functions, spiritual growth, and attending my alma mater in Michigan!

Then came the email when I was in Bosnia. Tara asked me to walk her down the aisle for her wedding. She specified that I had to wear my dress blue Army uniform. Tara's wedding invitation and participation became the ultimate reward for my simple compassion for a young lady in need of a father.

INFLUENCE #17

JIM ROBERTS was instrumental in the founding of Calvary in 1973. He was a deacon when I became Calvary's fifth pastor.

Jim provided mature guidance and wisdom during deacon meetings and in personal conversations.

Jim and I were the first to survey the property where the Calvary facility is now located. I still remember the ride on his ATV. I think he was attempting to impress me with his "youthfulness" and driving ability! Frankly, he made me nervous.

After touring the property we stopped in the middle of the field and looked out over the valley, Interstate 81, and the local Route 11. As we enjoyed the view, we talked about how likely that exact spot would someday probably be the front entrance to the new church facility. We took time to pray that the Lord would allow us to buy the property. Literally, that spot is now exactly where Calvary's entrance is today!

Jim was a visionary by my side that day. I can still see his smiling face.

Jim became more important to my son Mark than I thought possible when I became pastor of Calvary.

Frankly, Mark was not excited about moving to Pulaski because back in Fonda he had become an excellent athlete and quite accomplished in track. He had successfully participated in several events. He began to have his own identity instead of just being known as Pastor Ferry's son.

The move to Pulaski was difficult for Mark. However, he did adjust over the first school year. He did very well in track and ultimately set a record of 56.7 seconds in the intermediate hurtles race on a quarter mile track.

At the end of his first year in Pulaski, I asked, "Mark who has become your best friend this year?" (I was thinking school friends.) His immediate response was "Jim Roberts!" I was quite surprised. I asked him for an explanation.

Mark elaborated, "I have been with Jim almost every week to play pool at the Springbrook Apartments. He has become my best friend." Jim had invited Mark to come over on Monday nights. They did play pool but his time and influence on Mark was intentional. His goal was to emotionally stabilize a young man. Little did I know this was happening.

I loved Jim for many reasons but his ministry in my son's life was the capstone of his personal influence of grace in my life.

LOIS ROBERTS (2018 eulogy) has left a lasting impact on multiple generations of the Roberts' family, members of Calvary Baptist Church, and this former pastor!

Lois witnessed the founding of Calvary in 1973. She was a member while these men pastored Calvary: Ronald Jones, Leonard Stom, Tom Weber, John Zesewitz, Allen Ferry, Ralph Niven, Tom Williamson, and presently, George Waggoner.

I cannot speak for the others but Lois certainly treated me like family. Lois and Jim provided "room and board" for me before our family moved into the Richland parsonage. Perhaps she adopted me because my age was close to her sons!

Last summer (2018), during a long phone conversation, we talked about the early days and the events surrounding the establishment of Calvary. Her memory was quite clear about the struggles and heartaches plus successes and joy! I truly enjoyed our last visit.

I also remember that the Ladies Trio usually included Linda Roberts, Vivian Hilton and Lois. Three wonderful women who each have contributed a lifetime of service to the Lord at Calvary.

Lois was a vital member of **The Starting Five** who helped build the new facility. Lois joined Bill Roberts, Chuck Laws, Erica Roberts, and Bob Ferry. Pastor Ken called them **The Starting Five** because they were present and ready to work virtually every day from March to November 1997. I can still visualize Lois and Erica operating the wood planer. She also stained all the doors and trim you see today in Calvary. Lois was not a snowflake! She was a worker.

The Starting Five
L-R Chuck Laws, Lois Roberts, Bob Ferry, Erica Roberts, Bill Roberts
(see Appendix, Article 11 Eulogy for Chuck & Anna Laws)

The two most difficult memorial services I have ever conducted were for Jason Jacobs and Jim Roberts. I remember Linda Roberts singing "Thank You" by Ray Boltz. I barely finished

Jim's service, went into the kitchen, and completely lost it emotionally.

I also remember the day of Jim's burial in the South Richland Cemetery in Fernwood. I honestly believe that Lois was stronger that day than I was. We shared that moment in the light rain with great confidence in our hope in Christ beyond the grave.

Now, many years later, I write with tears and blurred vision because I loved Lois and sadly recognize that the era of her influence has ended. This does not diminish anyone else still living or with the Lord… it is a fact. Lois was not perfect but very special as a wife, as a mother, as a church member, and as my friend!

Women of Lois's faith and stature are not plentiful. Calvary has been privileged to have her influence for 45+ years! We can certainly say that Lois was an active member of the Greatest Generation. She will be missed but never forgotten.

INFLUENCE #18

LINDA ROBERTS

Linda was the choir director during the ten years I was pastor of Calvary. Her ministry was a consistent and constant personal blessing to me and also the congregation.

I taught the Bible at Lamoka Baptist Camp for several summers. I used the daily free time to study the scripture, develop themes, prepare message outlines, and list suggestions for hymns. At the end of the camping week I would give the results to Linda.

I followed this practice for those four summers and even sang in the choir but I was always surprised when week after week the choir selection, special music, and congregational hymns matched up perfectly with the message. Linda had the spiritual discernment to match music with the message of the day.

Linda was not a talker. She was a doer, a worker, a consummate choir director and my friend. Linda's heart and mind were in her ministry of music.

Even tonight in choir practice I was thinking about Linda. Our choir director is outstanding. Little things he does reminds me of Linda. He is very good but the gold standard will always be Linda Roberts.

Honorable "Influence" Mention

Now, I know I risk breaking pastoral protocol by honoring some but not everyone. I trust that those not included will have deep enough spiritual maturity to be forgiving!

Vivian Hilton

Vivian started serving in the child-care nursery during the Nixon administration. Although he resigned, Vivian never has! She faithfully continues today as a choice servant.

Peggy Sawchuck

Peggy was the lady who often left encouraging notes for me on the pulpit. I remember her kindness. She was a pianist for the choir, soloists, trios, and other special music.

Bonnie VanDyke, Mary O'Brien Curcio & Jan Hays taught Sunday School for many years with classrooms which demonstrated both age-specific educational understanding, compassion for their students, and Biblical insight.

Cavalry Baptist?

LAUGH WITH ME — In 1997, a new county sign in Richland had a slight spelling error which created a new image for Calvary.

Folks thought about riding horses but they were already known for carrying their sabers (swords)!

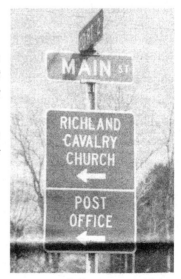

LAMOKA BAPTIST CAMP

For the four summers I was the Bible speaker for junior-age campers (ages 8-12). The camp became a very special place to our children: Mark and Julaine.

Julaine worked in Lamoka Snack Shack. It was her first job which later proved to launch her high school employment.

One summer the Director asked Mark to serve as a cabin counselor. This was the beginning of his long-standing ministry at Lamoka.

THINK WITH ME — Christian Camping was integral in the spiritual journey of our family. Theresa was a camper and counselor at Lamoka years before and during college. Julaine sold snacks, Mark counseled, and I cut grass but God had big plans for all of us. Camp was a place of grace!

Consider Christian Camping for your family!

PULASKI AREA HIGH SCHOOL GRADUATES

MARK graduated in 1990, and immediately went to Baptist Bible College. Originally, he started in a two year associates degree but within a few months he asked if he could transfer into the Youth Ministries program. We agreed. We were excited the direction the Lord was taking him.

JULAINE

With the military build-up for Dessert Storm, the NGB ordered me to join a Combat Construction Battalion out of Buffalo. During this time, Julaine asked me if she could consider leaving High School and enter college early? *(see Appendix, Article 6, Where Did the Time Go?)*

We discovered that she could leave high school and finish necessary courses in college. When she graduated from high school in 1991, she had already finished 41 college credit hours.

Baptist Bible College Graduates

Mark & Heather (future wife) graduated in 1994; Julaine in 1995.

Julaine also graduated from National Technical Institute for the Deaf, a college of the Rochester Institute of Technology in 1997.

FATHER & SON BANQUET MISSED

During Mark's senior year he did very well in the 400 meter high hurtles. His senior year goal was to break the Pulaski school record. An early groin pull set him back some but seemed in great shape for the qualifiers for the Empire State Games held on a spring Saturday afternoon in Liverpool.

I had drill that Saturday but with commander approval, I left early afternoon for the qualifiers. Diedra Johnson, Mark's personal trainer, was on hand. We were all very excited.

However, conflict happens! CBC's annual Father & Son Banquet was the same evening. (CBC alternated these banquets: Mother & Daughter, Mother & Son, Father & Son, and Father & Daughter.)

So, when it became obvious that Mark's event was running late (pun intended), I called the lady in charge to say that I would not be able to host the banquet. She was not happy! Pastor Ken took over.

Diedra and I watched with pride as Mark set the new school record of a 56.7 seconds! We did not attend the banquet but the three of us have a very special memory.

Throughout that afternoon I thought of Dr. Getz and how he left the service to watch his son in his last high school football game. His example made a significant impact on my life many years later!

PROPERTY & FACILITY CONSTRUCTION

For several years our service and class times were 9:00 to 10:10 and 10:30 to 11:40 but parking continued to be problematic. Our youth ministries, choir concerts, numerous banquets, and expository preaching drew many people to the ministries of Calvary. Actual seating became a problem.

Ultimately, the Deacons and Pastors recommended several proposals to the congregation. (This process took several months.) They included:

- To build a new facility central to the membership living near Pulaski, Sandy Creek, and surrounding areas.
- To sell the Richland property which included the church building and parsonage. A shared well complicated the division of the property.
- To utilize the Pulaski Area High School auditorium during the time between the property sale and the completion of the new facility.
- To increase the Senior Pastor's salary after the sale of the parsonage to appropriately cover his new cost of housing. Pastor Ken had already received this benefit years earlier.

Finding a suitably located property became my personal objective. I knew the best place would be on Route 11, north of Canning Factory Road. So, I went door to door asking if owners had any thoughts of selling adjacent empty lots! I found no interested folks.

THE LORD — THE ULTIMATE REALTOR

Julaine sadly called on August 13, 1990 from Camp of the Nations where she was a Leader in Training (LIT). Her friend Mike Ruddy had been in an auto accident. She asked if Mom and I would visit him in the hospital.

Theresa and I immediately traveled to St. Mary's Hospital in Watertown (NY) where we met Mike's mom and dad, Linda and Michael, Sr. Ruddy. It became the first of many visits.

During the following weeks, Michael and I had many serious conversations regarding spiritual matters. I also learned that they had moved to Pulaski just the previous year. When I asked the reason for relocation, I learned that they moved because Linda was the executor of her father's estate.

I had to ask, "Why will it take so long to settle your father's estate?"

Linda said, "Well, Dad owned several businesses and pieces of property."

I asked, "Would the properties include anything out on Route 11?"

Linda answered, "Yes, we own a farm on Route 11, the one with a large patch on the roof."

I calmly responded, "I'll have to take a look."

Mike did not recover from his injuries. He died on Monday, August 25.

Michael, Sr. asked me to speak at Mike's memorial service. He specifically requested that I tell Mike's classmates how to have a relationship with God.

I agreed. I spoke about the relatively "short" life of Enoch in Genesis. After the men's ages are proportioned, Enoch was only about 22 or 23 compared to the rest of those mentioned in Genesis chapter five. It is also noted later in Hebrews, "By faith Enoch was taken away so that he did not see death, and was not found, because God had taken him; for before he was taken he had this testimony, that he pleased God." (Hebrews 11:5)

A significant number of Mike and Julaine's classmates were present. Feedback was very positive.

True to her word, Linda called the following spring and offered Calvary the privilege to take what we wanted from that farm on Route 11. When the process was complete, we bought 20 acres from the "Ruddy" estate.

Julaine's concern for her friend Mike, led Theresa and me to the Ruddy's who became our friends in their time of grief.

Julaine's concern for her friend led us to the property which ultimately became the location for the new Calvary Baptist Church!

The Lord led us through Julaine's tender heart toward hurting hearts. Ministry in the Ruddy's lives was of utmost importance but the Lord also met the need of Calvary.

THE REST OF THE STORY

Julaine's initiated her friendship with Mike because he was a new student in Pulaski in the 1989-1990 school year; she was new in 1988-1989. She understood his situation. She also appreciated his unique faith. They connected on this spiritual level but personally we did not know Mike.

A few years later, Linda's sister moved to town and became friends with Theresa. She shared with us, that years earlier, Mike had spent vacation with her down south. During that time Mike attended a vacation Bible school and had come to personal faith in Christ.

Julaine's sensitive spirit had identified his spirit as the same.

FRIENDSHIP WITH DEACONS—ALL REFLECTIONS OF GRACE

During the years we ministered at Calvary, I served with several Godly deacons. We had "Maalox Free" Deacon Meetings. I always anticipated the meetings with these fantastic servants. Let me briefly tell you about these men alphabetically not by greater or less importance.

LARRY ATKINSON was a salesman for Pioneer Seed Products in 1988. His small farm was home for several Holsteins and a few deer! Larry and I shared a love for deer hunting and shooting sports in general. The Lord gifted him with a fantastic memory. His testimony was crystal clear.

Together we established the first Game Dinner in 1989. Larry, the chef, prepared all of the wild game and everything else. Our first dinner was held in the Elementary cafeteria. Over 200 folks attended.

Larry and I envisioned and helped build the pavilion near the pond.

HAROLD HAYS was an accomplished mechanic at a local farm tractor company. More importantly, Harold and Jan were faithful teachers in Sunday School. I really don't know who did the most teaching, probably Jan, but together they were a quality example for the children to see each Sunday. They claimed those children as their own.

JOHN JACOBS was mentioned earlier as the Chairman of the Deacons who made budgetary recommendations regarding pastoral salaries. But John's most memorable characteristic was his zeal for evangelism. For several years, together we did weekly visitation of church visitors and those known in need of encouragement. He also taught a Bible class on evangelism which led many members to be more effective witnesses.

Our church was deeply affected when Jason, John and Mary's young son, was diagnosed with Leukemia in 1988. Born on December 27, 1985, he died on April 27, 1995. Jason was Calvary's focus for prayer and family support during those years. He had a tremendous testimony in and out of the hospital.

I have forgotten the number of surgeries and procedures Jason endured but I remember John and Mary's faithfulness throughout the seven years of their son's illness.

I have one clear vision that is permanently etched on the canvas of my memory. As we stood in Evergreen Cemetery in Orwell on a slight slope, I can still see the many, many friends and family gathered around the Jacobs for Jason's internment.

Most significant is this fact, when Rich Steele, George White and I began to sing… almost immediately John joined us with these lyrics by Jim Hill:

There is coming a day,
When no heart aches shall come,
No more clouds in the sky,
No more tears to dim the eye,
All is peace forever more,
On that happy golden shore,
What a day, glorious day that will be.

There'll be no sorrow there,
No more burdens to bear,
No more sickness, no pain,
No more parting over there;
And forever I will be,
With the One who died for me,
What a day, glorious day that will be.

What a day that will be,
When my Jesus I shall see,

And I look upon His face,
The One who saved me by His grace;
When He takes me by the hand,
And leads me through the Promised Land,
What a day, glorious day that will be

STEVE JONES was an agricultural teacher for over 30 years. He brought a delightfully positive spirit and Biblical insight to the meetings and our church. He was the epitome of graciousness and kindness. I never heard a negative word from this true "gentleman."

ART POTTER was the quiet man at the deacon meetings. I had to draw out the wisdom that was deep in this man's heart and soul. I usually asked Art for his thoughts first before the others for two reasons. First, he would not normally speak unless I asked him directly. Second, I wanted the other men to hear him first because Art would set a quiet tone to our meetings that brought thoughtful responses.

Art was a blessing and we hated to see him and Liz relocate.

TOM ROBERTS was a very special man. I wrote the following eulogy for his too soon passing in 2011.

In 1988, when I came to candidate at Calvary Baptist Church, Tom was absent. He was on a school trip with his daughter. I looked at him as a deacon who actually had his priorities right.

Tom was a quiet but quality man. He built his own home for Linda, his queen, and his three princesses: Maria, Tove, and Misty.

He worked world-wide and long hours to provide for his family. He enjoyed hunting with brother Bill in southern tier at Laurie's folks' property. He loved Stillwater Reservoir with John and Mary Jacobs.

Tom influenced Linda's decision to accept Christ as Savior. Tom provided the basement where he, Linda, Jim, and Lois hosted Calvary and provided leadership for its early days.

Tom also provided an excellent example of friendship before, during and after Jason's seven year battle with Leukemia; of parenthood with imperfect children like mine; of more recent grand-parenting!

Tom helped build this ministry facility. However, years before, Tom helped build the foundation of this church. Tom's life demonstrated that he was saved to serve.

DAVE RUSSELL was the youngest deacon at Calvary but he brought significant insight to the table. Dave and Tammy worked with the youth for many years. I remember the praise the kids gave to them.

I also remember my first visit to their home in Parish. Immediately after getting out of my vehicle, Brad, their four or five year old son, took me by the hand and gave me a tour of "his" property. I can still see and feel Brad's grip on my hand and also my heart. Brad was deaf but that did not stop him from providing hospitality.

INTERESTING OBSERVATION

The Lord strategically placed a deaf child in both the Village Bible and Calvary Baptist churches. The Lord used these two young boys to touch Julaine's heart for deaf ministry and future vocation. After graduating from the National Technical Institute for the Deaf on the campus of Rochester Institute of Technology in 1997, Julaine traveled to Jamaica for many summers to work at the Caribbean Christian Center for the Deaf. This continued until 2006, when she also volunteered at an orphanage where she found Enoch.

DAN SAWCHUCK came to Calvary with a special heart for ministry. We met weekly at 6:00 a.m. for discipleship where I developed a high appreciation for this hard working husband and father.

RICH STEELE was the deacon who always had time to accompany me while delivering groceries to needy families. I remember one night we took loaves of bread and peanut butter to one couple with several children. They were clearly not appreciative. Rich kindly told them that many times bread and peanut butter was all he had in his home for his ten children!

JOHN TOOMEY was our dear neighbor in Richland. He was also the church treasurer for many years. John was another quiet man but often made profound statements. During one all-night mens prayer meeting, he wrote and presented an essay on pastoral support. He had me hold up a staff for many, many minutes. He then asked other men to help hold up the ends. As he talked on and on, he added more and men to support the staff as I was tiring. He painted, literally and figuratively, a vivid picture of pastoral support during times of weighty burdens.

LAUGH WITH ME — During one winter, John hung gallon milk jugs to taps in the maple trees that bordered his property on back of the church in Richland. Our son Mark came home from school one afternoon and announced, "John Toomey is a man of significant faith. He must think he can get milk out of those maple trees!

DICK VANDYKE was our deacon with a "famous" name. He was far more important to Calvary than just his name. Dick always brought mature wisdom to the meetings. He and his wife Bonnie were faithful teachers of children and godly example to several generations moving through their classes.

LAUGH WITH ME — During one morning service during the offering, an usher handed me a note I have never forgotten. Seems that we had a visiter named Julie Andrews! I asked her to stand and I introduced Dick VanDyke and Julie Andrews!

DOUG WIDRICK is one of the family men that Chuck Laws invited to church. *(see Appendix, Article 11, Chuck & Anna Laws Eulogy)* Doug quickly involved himself in the active church life of Calvary. When we built the pavilion, Doug and I picked up 260 plastic lawn chairs from the distributor. We used them in the new sanctuary until the permanent chairs arrived. Then they became the seating for the pavilion. Doug brought common sense and a strong work ethic to our leadership team. During the celebration for completing the facility in 1997, we gave Doug the MVP award in the employed category.

LAUGH WITH ME — I had one preaching blooper at Calvary that stopped the service. I was introducing the book of first Thessalonians. I said, "Paul's commendation for this church did not include the size or construction of the building, the size of the parking lot, or church polity because this church was more than an organization, this church was a living "orgasm." Whoops!

INFLUENCE #19

UNCLE BILL ROBERTS
EULOGY, 2005

Uncle Bill Roberts was a legend around Calvary Baptist Church for many years.

Uncle Bill was the white-haired man at the door to greet all ages and welcome them to Calvary.

Uncle Bill was the only Godly Gramps some younger children at Calvary have ever had.

Uncle Bill did better justice to those old-man sweaters than Perry Como did. Perhaps his sweaters were not in vogue but his kindness and friendliness were!

Uncle Bill always brought to church a warm smile, a firm handshake, and sincere faith.

Uncle Bill, to my knowledge, never taught a class or served in leadership but he lived faithfully as a model, an example to those who were privileged to know him, watch him, learn from him, and love him.

Uncle Bill was a significant member of the "starting five" during the construction of the Calvary Baptist Church facility during 1997 (Erica Roberts, Lois Roberts, Chuck Laws, Bob Ferry and Bill Roberts).

Uncle Bill missed very few days from start to finish. He arrived each day with a willing spirit, a strong sense of purpose, a strange sense of humor, a twinkle in his eye, and a wife who knew how to make outstanding lunches, particularly salads!

113

Uncle Bill worked on every room and every aspect of the building. If you see it, Uncle Bill probably touched it. And he did not have much time for those who stopped by to criticize and tell the "starting five" how to do something better!

In the 1970's I regularly traveled a country road in Massachusetts. At one place I always slowed to check an apple orchard on a hillside as I passed. Yes, I was looking for deer. Just above the orchard was one huge Old Oak appearing to stand on the horizon at the divide between heaven and earth. By the size and shape I would guess the Old Oak had been there for decades watching over the orchard and grazing deer.

The Old Oak was permanent, so it seemed, and most passing motorists probably took it for granted if they even noticed it. The seasons would come and go, so would the acorns and leaves, but the Old Oak was always there.

Years passed and late one afternoon I drove by and looked up to see if any deer were in the orchard, but something wasn't right. It took me a moment to figure out what was different and then I saw that the Old Oak was not there. I pulled over and realized a landmark was gone. Emotions overwhelmed me.

I thought of the first time I saw the Old Oak and the several deer feeding around it. I remember how it looked in the spring with fresh leaves, in the fall with bright colors, and in the middle of winter looking almost naked, anxious for the greenness of spring!

Uncle Bill has been like that Old Oak for many, but especially for family, close friends, and me.

Perhaps some who gather today to honor Uncle Bill took his presence for granted and now you really miss him. Perhaps some treasured his stature, his solid presence, his unassuming personality, and today you hurt deeply because of his absence.

Uncle Bill stood tall and solid for many decades. He demonstrated that true greatness is best measured by those who weather the storms of life and greet each new season with confidence and courage. Greatness is not flashy nor formal but relaxed and resilient.

Greatness for that Old Oak and Uncle Bill Roberts was determined by that which could not be seen by the natural eye. Both stood tall and solid because they had deep roots; roots which provided stability and sustenance. Roots were actually the origin of their outward appearance. The Old Oak had green leaves in the spring and acorns in the fall because of those deep roots. And they also provided strength for everyday survival.

Uncle Bill was a man of faith but not a faith without works. His faith had deep roots. His faith provided the source for his gracious life and hard work for the Lord.

Uncle Bill, like the Old Oak, stood for years on the horizon between heaven and earth. He was a landmark. And like the Old Oak, Uncle Bill Roberts is now gone. He has moved to heaven from earth. He crossed over the horizon into a land where the sun never sets!

A vivid mental video reminds me today of that Old Oak. Even more vivid, however, are the memories of Uncle Bill:

- *Arriving at the building each morning ready to work*
- *Standing by the front doors of Calvary Baptist with a warm smile, a welcome handshake, and a Church Bulletin*
- *Setting up tables for Church dinners*
- *Enjoying the desserts*
- *Modeling Christian maturity for another generation*
- *Embarrassing Abetta on a regular basis!*

I hold these memories as precious reminders of my friend, Uncle Bill Roberts.

Join me, deepen your roots, stand tall, and do justice to the heritage he has left us.

RUSS & BECK WING

Reference Letter
31 October 2006

I know Russ and Beck Wing as former members of Calvary Baptist Church in Pulaski, NY, where I was Senior Pastor (1988-1998). Wings were members of the church when I arrived and later Russ served as a deacon and a regular teacher before leaving for Practical Bible College (now Davis College).

Friends. *I would describe my relationship with Russ and Beck as close friends. I have known them for over 18 years. The times I have been a guest in their home are too numerous to count. I have known their children from childhood into adulthood. I have current digital photographs of all their families in my computer and rejoice when each grandchild is born. Their joy has been my joy and their heartaches have been mine. I have received more communication and care packages from the Wings during three deployments than any other family and almost all others combined! I have hunted deer successfully on the Wing farm numerous times. (Russ and I are serious deer hunters.) My wife and I count Russ and Beck among our dearest friends.*

Parents. *Russ and Beck have significant parenting skills. Endowed by the Lord with unusual Biblical insight and balanced perspectives Russ and Beck have raised four godly children who have likewise chosen four godly mates. Russ and Beck are now enjoying third generation blessings. It will take a while to see how the grandchildren turn out but my guess is that each one of them will ultimately learn to love and serve the Savior from the influence of their parents and grandparents! Molly, Carrie, Brandon, and Trudy were fine examples for their peers during high school and continue as such! Russ and Beck are outstanding parents.*

Elder. *I had the privilege of watching Russ transform from a sheep into a shepherd. His wisdom was always sought and almost always welcome! From time to time Russ would shock the other deacons with convictions higher than theirs — thus not always welcome — however his grace was immeasurable in each presentation. Russ has knowledge and understanding that provide him with the capability to give wise counsel to those he shepherds. Russ is a man of mature wisdom thus I identify him as an elder!*

Bishop. *I have not witnessed Russ as an administrator of a local church. Therefore I cannot appropriately attest to his abilities as the overseer of a local assembly. I was proud to serve as the moderator of his ordination council. Several deacons testified of his skills as bishop.*

Teacher. *I have observed Russ as a teacher over the several years I have known him. Russ loves both the living Word of God and the written Word of God. He handles the scriptures with utmost respect and presents it as the authoritative inspired, inerrant, and infallible Word of God. Russ is a fine teacher.*

Preacher. *I have heard Russ preach several times and I would have to describe him as a pastor-teacher more than a preacher. He will ably feed a congregation, but I believe Russ' pulpit style is primarily as a teacher. However, I admit I have not heard him preach regularly.*

Beck. *Perhaps a word about "Beck" is appropriate. Other than the pencil normally seen over ear for musical score notation — Beck is just about flawless. I have never seen her ruffled nor in any emotional instability. Beck is an outstanding help-meet, mother, mother-in-law, daughter, deacon's wife, cookie-baker, pianist, and pastor-encourager! I know. Beck always encouraged me when some Sundays were a real challenge. I intentionally hung around Beck because she always had a good word and a smile. Honestly, if I didn't sound like I was over-doing it I'd say I think she must have wings! And since she came off the farm she looks younger than ever, even her hair looks younger!*

Church Membership. *While discerning the Lord's direction in their lives, Russ and Beck pursued church membership at West Genesee Hills Baptist Church in Camillus, NY. I know the fine pastor of this church has enjoyed the Wings involvement and attendance in the new-members class. The pastor teaches the class and has told me how special it is to have them participate in the class with insight and wisdom. The pastor is my son and has known the Wings for as long as I have!*

Wrap Up. *I believe the Wings have much to offer the right congregation. They are a solid, Biblical, loving, and fun couple with excellent credentials as teacher, parents, and friends.*

Eulogy June 1, 2014

Dear Becky, Immediate Family, Church Family, and Friends,

Writing about Russ is not a difficult task; knowing him was a wonderful and varied experience.

- *In church ministry he refreshed us all like a fresh breeze on a hot summer day.*
- *In thinking he demonstrated a complex mind as diverse as the glorious colors of fall.*
- *In confidence he navigated life as optimistically as he would plant a spring garden.*
- *In empathy he radiated warmth like a wood stove during a cold New Hampshire winter!*

Russ was exactly this: a man spiritually equipped to serve and minister during all seasons! However, Russ was far more than the sum total of his intellect, talents, abilities, and spiritual giftedness, he also possessed a sensitive heart in harmony with the will of His Lord and Savior.

Russ embodied Biblical values and virtue gained by constant and consistent exposure to the Word of God and his walk with the Lord Jesus. His study of the Word was unending. His devotion to the Lord was unwavering. His commitment to his church was unfailing. His example to his family was unequaled.

Yes, Russ was a pastor but he was a farmer when we first met in 1988. He was also a deacon who never missed church. He let me hunt deer on his farm; I really appreciated this man.

However, what impressed me most about Russ was his love for his wife and children. When I observed their interaction, their work ethic, their church involvement, their joyful spirit, their humble living, and their ultimate choices of spouses... I recognized that their father's leadership had set the right course for their adulthood and individual parenting.

In 2005, while thinking about Russ, I wrote the following from Proverbs 19:22.

What is desired in a man is kindness,
*   And a poor man is better than a liar.*

Poverty over Pretense

He once owned his own grocery store, then his own dairy farm. He walked into our lives wealthy by most standards; he left poor. Yet his life was marked with kindness not the pretense of prestige, power, or position; his heart was truthful, his actions were kind.

His were helping hands: calloused from labor but tender with kindness. An open home was an extension of his open heart: always room at his table for the lonely, the seedy, and the needy.

His earthly possessions were few. His life was an open book: his neighbors respected him, his church appreciated him, his family loved and honored him.

And ultimately God chose him for ministry! Today folks call him, "Pastor."

Principles for Application

- *Kindness and truthfulness are desired characteristics.*

- *Poverty is a baseline platform for ministry.*
- *Truth is preferred over pretense (lies).*

Prayer

Lord, thank You for those who are kind and for those who are transparent in truthfulness.

Lord, may we realize that our position in life becomes our platform for ministry; with or without, we have opportunity to serve You.

Give us wisdom, Lord, to understand this. Whether a corporal or a colonel let us be kind and truthful.

[Devotionals from Proverbs originally appeared in Allen's "Faith for the Forces" column in the Independent Baptist Voice, 2004-2005.]

How can we think of life without Russ Wing? Only by the sustaining grace of God can we continue our pilgrim journey as he so well modeled. Russ is now enjoying all that for which he invested his life: the legacy of a life lived for Christ and the anticipation of eternity together with the Lord and our brothers and sisters in Christ. His retirement benefits are truly out of this world!

I will never forget Russ Wing: my brother, my friend and fellow servant.

May the Lord bless and keep you, Becky, Molly, Carrie, Brandon, Trudy, your spouses, and your precious children.

Sincerely,

"Doctor Doug" (as Russ called me) and Theresa Ferry

Final Days at Calvary

We completed the 10,000+ square foot Calvary facility in 1997. Total building costs were $226,000 or $26 per square foot which included 300+ individual chairs from Bertolini Inc. and complete carpeting. We had our facility dedication with Reverend Chuck Little.

I was very tired from doing triple duty during 1997: pastor, chaplain, and construction manager. I started just about every day at 7:00 a.m. on the building site. I did sermon preparation and visitation during the evenings until after 11:00 p.m. The total result was that I was very tired.

During that year, Pastor Ken assumed all office hours and held down the day to day operations in Richland. He was also tired.

Pastor Ken resigned in November of 1997, to assume a new ministry in Maryland. Calvary was not the same without Ken and Vicki.

In 1997 and 1998, the Lord began to work on my heart regarding prison ministry; more on that to follow.

Calvary Baptist Church "Where the Pastor & People Care"
25th Anniversary Year 1973-1998 • Dr. Douglas Ferry, Pastor
5353 U.S. Rte 11 • Pulaski, NY 13142 • 315-298-6107

122

PART SIX

CORRECTIONAL CHAPLAINCY

1999-2012

STARTING POINT

I submitted the following document to the New York Department of Correctional Services as part of the application process. I include this to demonstrate that New York Department of Correctional Services has a process for hiring new chaplains. This process permits a wide variety of denominational men and women to enter prison ministry. As in every community, denominations have a difference in quality representation. This is just reality more than criticism. Let me quickly say that in my opinion, the best chaplains were not of my ecclesiastical or theological background. In view here is a personal calling to this ministry. (Inmates see a calling to ministry as more important than academic credentials; see *Insights from Inside: Chaplaincy & Corrections.*)

CALL TO CHAPLAINCY, 1998

I believe the Lord is leading me to minister in a correctional setting. I will briefly explain.

I invested two weeks in 1997 (8/23 to 9/6) supporting the Annual Training of the 2nd/108th Infantry Battalion of the 27th Brigade (NYARNG). During the 21 field services, not a few, but several correctional officers [also in the National Guard] commented that I should consider becoming a correctional chaplain. I had never thought about this ministry before! They explained the positives and negatives. I talked at length with these men. I was very moved by the need of the inmates and this raised my interest immensely.

Back home I visited confidentially with a long-time member of my church and good friend who is a correctional officer. I asked him what he thought about my ministry potential in the setting of a prison. He responded with enthusiasm and was eager to help me with finding out more information. He told me he thought several times about me becoming a prison chaplain but didn't mention it because he didn't want to lose me as his pastor! With his help I sent off a letter to Albany (9/20/1997).

I left the next day (9/21/1997) for the annual First Army Chaplains' Conference at Fort Dix. The first order of business was announced when the meeting began. "This morning we are going to have a VIP tour of the New Jersey Mid-State Corrections Facility here on Fort Dix." I couldn't believe it. I had never been inside a correctional facility. That day (9/22/1997) we had a tour and three-hour comprehensive briefing by three chaplains and several administrators. I was absolutely amazed by the timing of these events! And again I was moved by the complex needs of the inmates.

At a Bible conference (4/20/98), an illustration involved an old friend now with the Lord. The story revealed that his personal encounter with God, and the beginning of a new life in Christ, took place while incarcerated. I did not know this! Two of his sons are now in ministry.

Moved by the need, I volunteered one day per week at the Watertown Correctional Facility (NY). Chaplain Robert Durham mentored me for four months (2/98 to 5/98). What a tremendous privilege and learning experience. I participated in Prison Fellowship seminars, counseling, leading services, block visitation, and preaching. During that time I tasted just about all the various administrative paperwork.

I was a happy pastor of a wonderful church in Pulaski (NY) for ten years. I declined several pastoral and one college administrative (VP of Student Affairs) opportunities in recent years. I was settled in my ministry but when a calling to a new ministry became this obvious, I had to pursue the opportunity to confirm the Lord's leading.

My ministry gifts are preaching, writing (several published articles), and administration. I have a compassionate heart and was deeply involved with my church family. I rejoiced with those who rejoiced and wept with those who wept (Romans 12:15). I worked through complex matters with great detail.

I believe I must have a calling to serve in any high demand ministry. Quitting is too easy for those "doing ministry" for any other reason. The incarcerated have spiritual needs that are shared by all humanity, but their need is intensified by their circumstances. I want to channel God's grace into people's lives. God seems to be leading toward a prison ministry. I am certain God has something in store for me.

In May of 1998 the National Guard Bureau asked me to consider a 270 day tour of duty in Bosnia. When I inquired with the NYS Community of Churches regarding the status of my application, they informed me that they would have no known vacancies until spring of 1999. New Jersey was in a hiring freeze, so I accepted the opportunity to serve my country in this unique peace keeping mission.

I am scheduled to return in early April, but have permission to leave if and when an employment opportunity arises in a correctional setting. I continue highly motivated to enter a correctional facility and make a difference in the life of an individual, his/her family, and society — by the grace of God.

EPILOGUE — I resigned from the pastorate in summer of 1998 before leaving for Bosnia. I was fully confident that the Lord would put me into a prison ministry in His timing. When I returned from Bosnia in 1999, my earned leave (vacation) ended on April 21. On April 22, I began my ministry at Marcy Correctional Facility. The Lord gave me a seamless transition from the Pastorate, to Bosnia, and into Correctional Chaplaincy ministry. God is certainly good.

MARCY CORRECTIONAL FACILITY
1999-2004

Ministry at Marcy was a great experience for the most part. The first blessing was the Deputy of Programs who hired me. Deputy Nichols was a great guy who supported my chapel program.

Most security officers were respectful, some were not.

Inmates came in all types. Sadly, many of the Protestant Congregation were very disappointed that the Department did not hire an African American like the former chaplain. I learned quickly that racism is not of one color!

I quickly established myself by preaching the Word and the day by day demonstration of compassion toward everyone!

LAUGH WITH ME — While speaking on the subject of treating older women as your mother, younger women as your sister... I paused and said, "If you plan to break into my home and harm my wife or daughter... wear your best suit because you'll be laid out in it come morning!" When I came into the prison the next day the Captain asked if I had said what I said. Seems it was the talk of the yard the night before.

I started in April of 1999 and a new inmate arrived during that summer. He had a unique appearance with long blonde hair and mustache. He attended services and appeared interested but restless at the same time.

ERNIE SCOTT was friendly and talkative. He came from upstate New York. He was a Vietnam Veteran, church member, and Sunday school teacher. We had much in common. Ernie, however, was not certain about his relationship with the Lord. He came to truly know the Lord one night during a Bible study led by a volunteer. Exciting!

I baptized Ernie and discipled him on Sunday nights in my office.

Another rewarding ministry was the Bible Doctrine Class I taught using *Major Bible Themes* by Lewis Sperry Chafer. Ernie was one of my students, a great student. He completed the whole course with excellence.

Eventually Ernie transferred to an upstate prison and good volunteers were there to encourage him. He paroled in 2009. He immediately met up with the volunteers and participated in the establishment of a new church in Malone. Ernie has been a faithful member and participant.

I am very proud of my friend, Ernie Scott.

LAUGH WITH ME — One night in a sermon talking about the lure of forbidden fruit, I said, "If the grass is greener on the other side of the fence it may be caused by a backed up septic system." No one got it because everyone in chapel was from the five boroughs of NYC... except Ernie! He was the only one laughing. He laughed more and more as I tried to explain what a septic system was.

AUBURN CORRECTIONAL FACILITY
2004-2012

We moved from Pulaski to Marcy in 2002. We bought a nice home but each Sunday Theresa and I traveled to Camillus to attend our son's church. We did this for a several months.

Theresa and I were thinking of moving to Camillus when I learned that the Protestant Chaplain at Auburn had retired. I immediately called the NYS Director of Protestant Chaplains. I asked if I might transfer. She called back the next day and approved the transfer if the Deputy of Programs would agree.

I meet with the Deputy and he agreed. I was ready to start at Auburn when the New York Army National Guard notified me that I had to deploy again in support of Operation Iraqi Freedom III.

My next visit with the Deputy was sad because I was on staff for only a few days. However, the Department was required to hold my position in the event of a mandatory military deployment.

I returned from Iraq and resumed my ministry at Auburn. I remember that I rode my motorcycle the first day and parked in the designated lot.

Later in the day, a security Lieutenant came by and introduced himself. I asked how he knew who I was. He answered that the word was spreading that the new Protestant Chaplain just returned from combat and rode in on a motorcycle! Hunting pictures of elk and many deer on my wall got his attention. That day and many times in the future officers would stop by for coffee and conversation.

Chapel was an interesting worship experience. Because the majority of the men were African-American, I accepted their gospel style of music. Frankly, I enjoyed most of their selections. They in turn learned to appreciate my preaching style or for some... endure it.

Auburn men became very special to me for a variety of reasons; many contributed to my book, *Insights from Inside: Chaplains & Chaplaincy* (available on Amazon). I will repeat here what I included as biographic information on each of them. I retired in 2012, but when I think about Auburn, these are the men who immediately come to mind.

ALBERT was my tireless and flawless clerk. His work ethic was above reproach. His dedication benefited all congregations. (Albert will be released in December of 2019.)

BERNARD recently had his 79th birthday. I cannot begin to explain his significant encouragement to me during my years as his chaplain. Our conversations were extremely interesting, varied, detailed, and always respectful. His letters now have the same distinctive trademark of his keen mind, wit, and wisdom. I miss our face-to-face conversations!

CHRISTOPHER suggested the title for my last book. I believe that *Insight from Inside* captured the intent of what I wanted my students to learn: the qualities of a good chaplain. (Chris will be released this fall.)

DENNIS came into the chapel ministry through my small involvement in the Veteran's Organization. He became a regular and consistent part of the Protestant Community. He regularly appeared in my office armed with deep questions about Biblical subjects. Ultimately, Dennis bought a good Study Bible, took numerous correspondence courses, and became a great student of the Word of God. I am proud to call him my friend.

EDWARD was a highly respected member of our Protestant community. With respect came responsibility. He never backed away from what he said he would do. Ed was one of a few who had the total ministry in his heart and prayer. I miss my friend and our conversations.

JOHN has a keen mind and heart for the Lord. He is the only Lutheran I have known in prison. Either few Lutherans are criminals or they just don't get caught. His challenging discussions were always respectful and insightful into deeper theological issues.

LAWRENCE is a devoted Muslim, Vietnam Veteran, and my good friend. With great respect I watched his perseverance through extreme medical issues and the death of his wife. I miss our conversations.

MICHAEL brought significant musical skills to our chapel band but his outstanding example of spiritual growth in Christ and desire to improve himself in order to help others make him a very special man.

PAUL is articulate and an excellent writer. His insights reveal his depth of understanding of the Word of God, chaplaincy, and corrections.

ROBERT was released a few years ago and is now serving on staff of a New York City church. "Pops" was the spiritual leader of the Auburn Protestant Chapel during my eight years as his chaplain. He was a Godly man who regularly influenced others in their walk with the Lord. His past was despicable but through the grace of salvation, forgiveness, his surrender to God, and progressive sanctification... Robert's testimony in Christ is now flawless.

THOMAS came with his former Chaplain's blessing who said that Tom was a BOFA which I asked the Chaplain to define. He said that Tom was a "Breath Of Fresh Air" (which is in short supply in the prison context). Tom proved to be just that, a BOFA.

I can use this picture now that these two men have been released. Robert and Ernie both have my utmost respect. Robert is on staff at a NYC church and Ernie works in Florida for the VA as an advocate for homeless veterans.

PART SEVEN

MILITARY DEPLOYMENTS

HEAVY DECISION

In the spring of 1998, I had a strong burden toward prison ministry. However, NYS and NJS Department of Corrections were not currently hiring chaplains. They said that it might be six to ten months before they would be hiring again.

I should mention that I had shared with the deacons how the Lord was leading me toward a prison ministry. I told them that it might be several months before an opening would be available. I suggested that the men give some thought about starting the process of looking for a new pastor while I was still available to continue my pastoral duties. I was willing to be absent any time they wanted to have a candidate visit.

The lengthy discussion was summed up by a deacon's question, "When are you leaving?" Of course at that point I did not have a definite answer. After ten years with these men, the thought of my leaving was both hard on them and me.

The same week I received a call from the National Guard Bureau (NGB) asking if I would do a nine-month deployment to Bosnia. NGB was actually looking for three chaplains. Initially I thought I did not want to leave Calvary this soon. I suggested to NGB that a friend might be interested and I told them that I would connect with him.

Later that week I went to Fort Drum for training. Fort Drum was about 40 miles from my home in Pulaski. I arranged to meet and have dinner with my friend, Chaplain Joe Weidler. I thought he might be interested in the deployment. However, he told me that he could not for family reasons.

Honestly, I was very emotional about the decision I was about to make. I was awake almost the whole first night at Fort Drum praying while seeking the Lord's direction. I remember taking two or three showers and praying some more.

By morning I knew I could not keep Calvary on hold for several months and that the nine-month deployment might be the clean break needed for the deacons to start the pastoral search process.

I was in constant contact with Theresa about this new ministry direction.

I gave notice of my resignation that Sunday.

BOSNIA-HERZEGOVINA

Going to Bosnia was a two-step process. First, I had to travel through Fort Benning (GA). Because my National Guard medical records did not arrive earlier, I had to take a full battery of inoculations and repetitive blood work. Records did arrive one day too late!

One practical field exercise taught us how to probe for landmines while crawling in the sand in 100 degree heat. It was fun! Right.

The trainers continually said, "If you did not drop it, don't pick it up!" They were preparing us for the real-world of landmines which were just about everywhere in Bosnia.

I landed in Tuzla, Bosnia in August. Climate was about the same as New York. Summers were pretty warm. Winter brought snow and cold about the same as back home.

I assumed the position of Deputy Chaplain for the 1st Armor Division. My office was in the White House on the air force base outside of Tuzla. The main three-story building was white and housed the primary staff of the 1st Armor Division and later the 1st Cavalry Division.

Initially I worked for Chaplain Rogers and later for Chaplain Erkkinen. I enjoyed learning from these men with many years of active duty experience.

At my first chaplains meeting, the senior chaplain delegated the preaching responsibilities of various chapels. I began to preach in the General Protestant Chapel every Sunday. I also agreed to supervise the Gospel Congregation, little did I know the blessing those folks would be!

We used Pegasus Hall for Sunday Services. This was a non-designated space and I had to reserve it every week. Otherwise, it could be used by any group. This became problematic almost immediately in the person of the "Mayor" of our community. Although we ultimately had a good relationship — at first we locked horns! Then he said, "Chaplain, get the funds and build a chapel." Okay, I like a challenge. More on this later.

The Gospel Congregation became my favorite assignment because of the fine folks I met there. They treated me with honor and respect but more than this was the quality of the men and women who gathered at Pegasus Hall on Sundays at 1400 hours (2:00 p.m.).

The military does recognize and makes provisions for religious groups with unique worship requirements. These include Mormons, Jews, Episcopalians, Catholics, Greek Orthodox, etc. General Protestants and Gospel Congregation are two groups which are the catch-all for remaining Protestants.

General Protestants attract the major denominations like Methodists, Baptists, Presbyterians, and a wide variety of lessor groups. I preached in this congregation for several weeks. Some very fine people worshiped during this service.

Gospel Congregations attract a wide variety of church members, folks who perhaps have Pentecostal persuasions or specific musical distinction. This congregation was significantly African-American. However, I was accepted because I preached the Word. This was greatly appreciated by the Gospel Congregation.

Gospel Congregations are authorized to choose their own "Pastors." I heard some fantastic preaching by non-chaplain military personnel.

Note that I said, "non-chaplain" rather than "not qualified" personnel. I heard phenomenal preaching and teaching by these Godly folks. From my viewpoint, many of these men were more qualified than many of the chaplains. It is a calling and spiritual giftedness that make one qualified; not a degree, ordination, or military commission.

On 7 October 1998, the 1st Cavalry Division assumed authority of the Multinational Division (North) area of operations in Bosnia-Herzegovina from the 1st Armored Division. I remember it was on my 51st birthday.

INFLUENCE #21

RICK PINA

With the change of command came one perfect example of a man called and gifted by God. Working in the communications section, WO1 Rick Pina was a man on a mission.

The sermons I heard Rick preach were amazing. Rick's introductions had more content than most total sermons I have heard. His messages were always text oriented, personally appropriate, and engaging.

When the time came, Rick asked me to assist in his promotion to CWO2. I was pleased that he asked me. Rick was quickly becoming a very special friend.

The Gospel Congregation has traditions. One is that the ministers sit in the front row. I was instructed where I was to sit... next to Mr. Pina.

With 1st Armor preacher gone, the Division Chaplain asked me to recommend the next Pastor for the Gospel Congregation. Only one person had the qualifications for a good ministry. I recommended Rick.

LAUGH WITH ME — During one service, Rick leaned over and said that the Lord had revealed the lady he should consider for his wife. I asked, "What does she think of this idea?" He answered, "I don't know, I haven't told her yet."

Rick and Isabella are now married and have a vibrant ministry.

Many years later, Rick invited me to the Pentagon to witness his final military promotion to Chief Warrant Officer Five (CWO5).

SARAJEVO

In January 1999, I was responsible for a chaplaincy meeting in Sarajevo. The first week, we pulled half of the Unit Ministry Teams (UMT) from all Multinational Division (North) camps and half the second week. We did not want to leave our camps without chaplains.

Sarajevo was the sight of the 1984 Winter Olympics, officially known as the XIV Olympic Winter Games which took place in February 1984. I was shocked by the before and after sights I witnessed: beautiful ski slopes but barbed wire everywhere!

A walk downtown permitted me to see the Sarajevo Roses which were concrete scars caused by a mortar shell's explosion that were later filled with red resin. Mortar rounds landing on concrete create a unique fragmentation pattern that looks almost floral in arrangement.

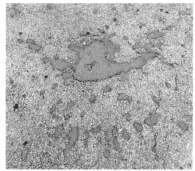

Throughout the city, explosion marks have been filled with red resin to mark where mortar explosions resulted in one or more deaths.

CWO5 BILL ROSSER encouraged me by singing in the evening service and his odd but great sense of humor. We still are in touch. We met up in in Texas in 2016 and enjoyed renewed fellowship.

EAGLE WINGS CHAPEL was my final physical project. I designed the floor plan (Power Point) after I surveyed the other chaplains to incorporate their ideas. I made the proposal to the commanding General Byrnes. He signed off on the $93,000 cost.

I was there at the right time to design and fund a place of worship for the soldiers on Tuzla Base although the chapel was built after I redeployed.

This was a great experience for my first deployment.

GROUND ZERO, 2001

I began ministry at Marcy Correctional Facility in 1999 and continued with the Army National Guard.

On Tuesday, 9/11, I was in my office when Theresa called to tell me an airplane had hit one of the Twin Towers in NYC.

I immediately ran down to the gym lobby and asked them to turn on the TV. We watched as the second airliner hit the second tower.

Soon thereafter, Chaplain (COL) Jake Goldstein, called me to report for duty at the Park Avenue Armory at 643 Park Avenue, New York, NY 10065. This was the Head Quarters of the Task Force Rainbow Hope.

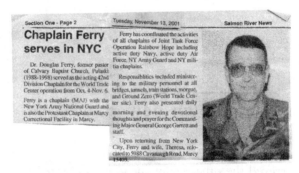

Section One - Page 2 — Tuesday, November 13, 2001 — Salmon River News

Chaplain Ferry serves in NYC

Dr. Douglas Ferry, former pastor of Calvary Baptist Church, Pulaski (1988-1998) served as the acting 42nd Division Chaplain for the World Trade Center operation from Oct. 4-Nov. 6. Ferry is a chaplain (MAJ) with the New York Army National Guard and is also the Protestant Chaplain at Marcy Correctional Facility in Marcy.

Ferry has coordinated the activities of all chaplains of Joint Task Force Operation Rainbow Hope including active duty Navy, active duty Air Force, NY Army Guard and NY militia chaplains.

Responsibilities included ministering to the military personnel at all bridges, tunnels, train stations, morgue, and Ground Zero (World Trade Center site). Ferry also presented daily morning and evening devotional thoughts and prayer for the Commanding Major General George Garrett and staff.

Upon returning from New York City, Ferry and wife, Theresa, relocated to 5988 Cavanaugh Road, Marcy 13403.

CHAPLAIN BOB TILLI (right) and I daily visited troops and civilians at Ground Zero. Bob is a chaplain for both the Air Guard and Veterans Administration.

MG THOMAS GARRETT was the commander at Ground Zero for Task Force Rainbow Hope. In 2004, General Garrett promoted me to LTC. His friendship continues today. A few years ago we did a motorcycle ride to the Harley-Davison plant in York, PA.

MEMORY FROM TRAINING AT FORT DRUM

LAUGH WITH ME — One year on the rifle range with Chaplain Bill Leone, I made an offer to a rifle company of 60+ men that we would excuse anyone who could out shoot me. When the smoke settled, I had 38 hits of 40 targets — one beat me and two tied with me — Bill and I then had the largest service attendance we ever experienced at Fort Drum!

OPERATION IRAQI FREEDOM I, 2003

The National Guard Bureau (NGB) contacted me in spring 2003, and asked me to join the 211th Military Police which was already deployed in Iraq. Their chaplain could not deploy. The Department of Defense position requires that every deployed battalion will have a chaplain.

LAUGH WITH ME — On my last working day before deploying as I was leaving the lobby and saw that it was set up with cake and ice cream. I thought to myself, "Is this for me?" As I ate a piece of cake, the Deputy began his speech. "We are here today to honor those who are retiring!" Most of the fine retiring folks were 55 years old. I was 55 and going to war!

I remember the flight into Kuwait. The pilot asked me to pray before landing. That was a surprise and privilege.

When I stepped into the 110 degree temperature at 0100 hours, I immediately felt the huge contrast with the 75 degree, air-conditioned cabin. The was the first taste of the summer heat.

SFC FRED COE met me at the airport where our friendship began. He became my escort to join up with the 211th in LSA Anaconda, Balad, Iraq.

Before we left Kuwait, Fred and I met General Myers and had a "photo op."

Time in Kuwait ended with a painful 350 mile trip upcountry in a Hummer, the longest two-day trip of my life. Hummer seats have very little padding and I certainly have very little!

We stopped along the way for fuel and rest. Because vehicles were coming and going all night, I elected to sleep under a Hummer. Others did the same.

Exiting the vehicle later on the second day, I could hardly walk. At 55, my back was sending me messages of crisis! I did survive and recovered.

The 211th MP Battalion was the HQ control of numerous companies from various states like Ohio, Florida, etc.

Fred provided size 13 dessert boots and cold Orange Crush from his private supply. What a friend.

FALLUJAH

I traveled on many operations with the 211th Commander, LTC Jack Hammonds. This photo was taken during a raid in June 2003. It has become my "Hoorah" picture from Operation Iraqi Freedom I.

Most days spent in Fallujah were non-eventful but one night provided an interesting story when we were ambushed. We did escape unharmed.

The next morning, Captain DeWitt and I checked out his vehicle and found that a round had gone through the cab. We looked closely and discovered the bullet was lodged in a roll of toilet paper.

Quilted Northern will stop bullets! These following pictures tell the story.

ARMS DEALER RAID

One day the 211th MP battalion orchestrated a raid utilizing numerous vehicles. I was with Commander Hammonds, his driver and the CSM when an Iraqi vehicle tried to escape. The Commander ordered the driver to force the enemy vehicle off the road. Two Iraqis jumped out of the truck bed and ran. The Commander and driver gave chase.

The CSM took a position off the front right door facing the area where the dealers were. I was positioned at the left rear door. With all the noice and confusion, I'm sure the CSM thought I was still in the Hummer and that the Commander and driver were chasing the only Iraqis. However, there were still three men in the cab of the small pickup less that 25 feet from me.

I did have access to a weapon but did not want to use it. About then a Hummer pulled up. A huge soldier exited and came over and said, "I have you covered, Sir."

He was very tall. As I looked up at the back of his helmet I saw that the Lord had sent a guardian angel. I needed not worry. He had etched on his helmet with a pen, "Safe in God's Hands."

LAUGH WITH ME — *One afternoon I was very hot and took an hour off. The temp was about 120 degrees. Not thinking about the time of day, I entered this shower point and turned the gravity water release valve from the black tank.*

The black tank had been sitting in the sun all day… the water was hot, extremely hot.

I exited looking like a lobster!

ADIRONDACK ADVENTURE

I returned from Iraq in October in time for northern zone muzzleloader deer season. Good friend Kemp Baratier invited me to hunt with him at a family camp in the Adirondacks. Kemp and I served together for many years in the National Guard.

The hunt was successful with great conversation, awesome campsite, super food, and a 212 pound buck. I sent the photo to Thompson Center and they put these pictures in the 2004 catalog.

WHAT RELIGION ARE YOU?

Soldiers asked me this question so many times that I wrote this track response, printed, and gave them out by the hundreds! My answers in brief:

I don't have religion, I have a relationship with the Lord:

1. This means receiving a Savior.
2. This means reading the Scriptures
3. This means responding in service.

OPERATION IRAQI FREEDOM III, 2004-2005

MOTORCYCLES I've had three great Hondas. This was my second: a 2004 Shadow 600. Mark and I enjoyed our too few rides together on identical machines before I left for Iraq.

LAUGH WITH ME — Years after we sold these Hondas, a dealer called about "my" Shadow. Seems that I had "Mark's" and Mark had "mine" all those years. We picked them up at the same time; the title serial numbers had been switched.

I was home from fall to spring when NGB activated the 42nd Division for Operation Iraqi Freedom III.

When I reported for the deployment process, a soldier from the personnel department looked at my records and said, "I see you were deployed for OIF-I."

I acknowledged his statement.

Then he continued, "Your first deployment was only five months and 15 days which means this deployment is mandatory — six months is the cutoff." I had no intention of declining but the option was not available.

INFLUENCE #22

CHAPLAIN SAUL CASTILLO

Saul was from California serving with an Aviation Battalion. He had one of the most congenial personalities I have encountered in uniform.

Saul is Seventh Day Adventist. He conducted his denominational services on Saturday. However, he assisted me on Sunday morning in my General Protestant Services. He would lead the music and help as necessary.

Although technically I was his supervisor, Saul needed no supervision! He was a blessing to me personally and to all troops of the aviation brigade, not only his battalion.

Throughout the week, Saul ministered in his battalion area. Troops loved him because he was a chaplain with a heart.

Saul's most recent duty station was the Joint Personal Effects Depot as a chaplain who met families of fallen military personnel returning to the states at Dover Air Force base in Delaware. I cannot think of a better person for such emotional duty.

I consider Saul as one of the finest chaplains I have known during my 21 years of service as a chaplain.

Thank you, Saul, for your great gracious influence on me in Iraq.

OIF-3 Unit Ministry Teams

INFLUENCE #23

CHAPLAIN JACKIE ANN ROSE KRAFT

As the NYS State Chaplain (2006-2008), I supervised all chaplains including Army National Guard, Air National Guard, and state militia.

Perhaps Jackie is now retired but I have never known a chaplain who could match her faithful service to the Lord and those to whom she ministered in the Air National Guard at the Niagara Fall Air Force Base.

Jackie was always busy but she found time to serve her local church congregation.

Her fellowship was encouraging. Her prayers were thoughtful. Her enthusiasm was contagious. Her smile was a blessing.

Influence #24

Chaplain Assistants

I have served with many chaplain assistants in the military. Some were good; some not. These three were outstanding!

John Monaco and **Allen Benningfield** were the epitome of combat assistants. Both were humble but confident; always busy but calm during stressful days; humorous but yet serious. Their love for the Lord was obvious and the desire to grow was admirable. They were servants as well as soldiers! We had lengthy conversations while we served together in Iraq. I watched as they served tirelessly in a combat area.

John and I flew one nighttime mission when something hit our Blackhawk. John thought we were going down! In darkness the literal "bird" hit seemed horrific!

Allen and I had many serious talks about his future and higher education. Since Iraq he has graduated from both college and graduate school. He is now married with a young son.

Curtis Street served with me stateside. We had outstanding times together. He could read maps, cook, drive, fish, and shoot. He could also finish my sentences and quote verses as I talked to soldiers about Christ. None better.

In Flight with SSG Monaco 2005

Preaching in Kuwait 2004

JAMAICA WITH JULAINE, 2006

Julaine loves the country and the people of Jamaica. She took Theresa on vacation over Christmas in 2004 while I was in Iraq.

When I returned in 2005, she asked me to visit Jamaica with her the following summer. So, we made plans for the first week of July to work at the Robin's Nest Orphanage.

My work objective was to build shelving for their new school classrooms. Julaine planned to generally do whatever she might do to be helpful.

Robin's Nest had almost 30 residents in July 2006. One boy, however, truly caught Julaine's eye and heart. Enoch was five months old when we first met. His birthday is February 2, 2006.

Enoch was significantly malnourished when the nest got him directly from the hospital when he was two months. However, he still looked bad but had added some weight. However he looked, Julaine fell in love with the little guy.

I have to admit that he was a happy kid but so were most of the other children. I did begin to enjoy time with him when I was not building 20+ shelving units.

I returned home after I finished up the carpentry projects. Within a few days, Julaine called. She asked if she were to adopt Enoch… would Mom and I help her. Sure, how hard could it be?

The adoption process out of Jamaica was very slow. Julaine made several trips for birthdays and paperwork. At one point the authorities told her that her fingerprints were not up to date! Think about that one!

I went with her in 2008, thinking we had it all done. Homeland security required more documentations and verification. We could not take him home! Leaving Enoch in Jamaica was the hardest thing I've ever done.

Returning in 2009 to Jamaica, Julaine and I were authorized to bring him home!

And the adventure began!

July 2006

August 2008

Age 13 on 2/2/19: 6'4" 205#, size 16 shoes

MOTORCYCLES This was my last Honda bought after my Army Retirement.

I rode this 1100 Shadow to work daily from March to November; 22 miles each way from Camillus to Auburn. It was a perfect way to relax after a long day in prison!

BILL PITCHER became a positive influence both spiritually and Biblically while on the road. Together we logged thousands of miles traveling the Adirondack Mountains in New England, the blue roads of Pennsylvania, and on the Tail of the Dragon from Tennessee to North Carolina. I miss those days and those rides.

Riding the Tail of the Dragon
Tennessee to North Carolina

PART EIGHT

MT. OLIVE BIBLE COLLEGE

2014-2016

In July of 2014, Dr. John Murdoch called me with a very special ministry opportunity in West Virginia. During the General Association of Regular Baptist Churches annual conference in Florida, Dr. Daniel Anderson, the president of Appalachian Bible College (ABC), asked John if he might know someone who would be qualified to establish and direct a Bible college inside a maximum security prison?

John recommended me!

Mr. Daniel Hanshew, the VP for Academic Affairs, spelled out the specific requirements:

1) Doctrinal agreement with ABC
2) Academic credentials to teach
3) Prison ministry experience
4) Work for a very low salary
5) Great personality

Well, four out of five isn't bad!

After the preliminary interview with Dan Hanshew, I returned for a second interview with Clarence Rider, the primary representative for the Commissioner of Corrections, and Calvin Sutphin, Founder of Catalyst Ministries which would financially underwrite Mt. Olive Bible College (MOBC).

I started in August of 2014. The same month, I visited the Angola Prison in Louisiana, the first prison with a successful "Seminary" operating. Angola was sponsored by New Orleans Baptist Theological Seminary. Although called a seminary, Angola is actually a four-year Bible college.

Read more about these ministries in my book *Insights from Inside: Chaplaincy & Corrections* which is available on Amazon.

I started the Mount Olive Bible College following the "Angola" model. We ran all classes concurrently. First year students took the same classes as the second, third and fourth year students. I would stack each class level with heavier assignments. Quite often I had the upper class men teach from their more comprehensive requirements the newer students.

I watched the men grow spiritually and in pastoral understanding. It was a joy to lead this ministry for the first two years.

MOBC is 222 miles from my home in North Carolina. The weekly round trip was exhausting. The second year I adjusted to modules and enlisted adjunct faculty to alternate with me.

During the first academic year (2014-2015) we held classes in a small space now used for the library.

INFLUENCE #25

CALVIN SUTPHIN II
CATALYST MINISTRIES, INC.

I have known very few men with the quality testimony that Calvin has developed since his conversion to Christ.

Calvin was a very successful business owner who came to know the Lord at a rehab facility less than ten years ago in 2009.

His conversion has been characterized by complete surrender. Upon returning home he sold most of his real estate holdings and stepped into full-time ministry. His purpose was to invest his finances with eternity in mind.

Calvin founded Catalyst Ministries, Inc. with the intent to bring moral rehabilitation to the correctional systems of West Virginia. I came to know Calvin when I agreed to direct the Bible College inside a West Virginia maximum security prison. Catalyst Ministries has paid all expenses for multiple ministries in addition to the college!

His vision came to fruition when the first class of Mt. Olive Bible College graduated earlier this year on January 22, 2019.

I am humbled to have had the privilege to work for and along side Calvin. He is a rare individual with deep commitment to do exactly what the Lord has given him to do.

AN HISTORIC OCCASION

Twenty-one inmates at Mount Olive Correctional Complex became the first graduating class of Mount Olive Bible College on January 22, 2019. A commencement ceremony in the maximum-security prison's gym featured remarks by Governor Jim Justice and Commissioner Betsy Jividen of the West Virginia Division of Corrections and Rehabilitation.

Eleven graduates were recognized for achieving highest honors (GPA 3.85-4.0), six for high honors (3.6-3.84), and two for honors (3.30-3.59). All twenty-one men, dressed in caps and gowns, crossed the stage to receive their diplomas. In keeping with Appalachian Bible College tradition, each graduate was also granted a Servant's Mantle—a symbolic towel printed with the words "Trained to Serve."

Mount Olive Bible College is an off site location of Appalachian Bible College of Mount Hope. The West Virginia Division of Corrections and Rehabilitation facilitates MOBC as a moral rehabilitation program. Appalachian Bible College and Catalyst Ministries partner to provide the donor-supported program at no cost to the students or taxpayers.

Jim Rubenstein, former Commissioner of Corrections, initiated the establishment of MOBC after hearing of the success of a Bible college within Louisiana State Penitentiary, also known as Angola. Beginning in September 2014, MOBC became the third program of its kind in the U.S.

Like Appalachian Bible College, MOBC is accredited by the Higher Learning Commission. All MOBC students major in both Bible/Theology and Pastoral Ministry, resulting in a Bachelor of Arts degree.

A sampling of required courses includes Bible Study Methods, Bible Doctrines, English Composition, Sociology, Apologetics, and Homiletics.

MOBC students must also participate in Field Service, which gives them regular opportunity to put into practice what they learn in the classroom. Field Service assignments include leading in chapel and Bible studies, and assisting in the library, medical ward, and mental health ward.

GLOBAL PRISON SEMINARIES FOUNDATION

Mt. Olive Bible College (classroom pictured above) is one of many colleges/seminaries which have been established inside maximum state prisons. The GPSF was formed to assist and encourage this national movement.

Dr. Kristi Miller and Ruth Graham recently toured the moral rehabilitation model being carried out by Catalyst Ministries in West Virginia. Ruth, the daughter of evangelist Billy Graham, has been a friend and supporter of the Angola Bible College for many years.

Catalyst Ministries is headed up by Calvin Sutphin II. Not too many years ago, Calvin made the visit to Angola and saw firsthand the impact of the moral rehabilitation model. He later returned home and asked himself, "Why not West Virginia?"

From there, he set out to establish a Bible College in the Mount Olive Correctional Center.

Calvin has started numerous initiatives to promote moral rehabilitation. He works with local law enforcement and is active in reentry projects that will provide employment training and opportunities to inmates and releasing inmates. Ruth and Kristi were so impressed with the amazing progress is such a short period of time. Ruth had this to say after the visit:

"I am still rejoicing in the work being done in West Virginia. The vision and the energy is so encouraging. I felt privileged to be there. The folks are terrific! I love the concept of the reentry program Calvin and Errol [law enforcement representative] have envisioned. It is inspiring. I can't wait to see it take shape."

Ruth Graham, Calvin Sutphin, Dr. Kristi Miller

Calvin Sutphin II

Part Nine

Books & Publications

(Available on Amazon)

A Man & His Country — *What does the Bible teach by example and principle about a man and authority? How do military service, war, and civil servanthood reconcile with God's Word? What does the Bible teach about politics? What does the Bible teach about civil disobedience? What about a man's responsibility as a citizen of Heaven? This 8-chapter study will help you discover what the Bible teaches about these issues and more. A Man and His Country will challenge you to be the kind of citizen God wants you to be.*

Wisdom for Warriors — *60 devotionals from Proverbs delivered to the Aviation Brigade while deployed for Operation Iraqi Freedom III.*

Threads of Family, Faith & Flag — *Allen Ferry and co-author Greg Masiello are combat veterans who served together during Operation Iraqi Freedom (2004-05). This book was conceived when they recognized that their shared patriotism was birthed from generational love for family, faith and the flag. They write from personal experiences that shaped their lives for military service. Journeys have been different but both are thrilled that their fellowship is based on a personal relationship with the Lord.*

They hope your patriotism will be increased as you travel with them from their home towns, get to know their families, live through Iraq, and into retirement.

Insights from Inside: Chaplaincy & Corrections — *"This insightful and personal treatment of prison ministry and Chaplaincy maintains a spiritual edge and is grounded in reality and honesty. It is a compilation of resources and vignettes from many sources that adds to its effectiveness. Bottom line of all the contributors is that Chaplains in correctional settings need to "keep it real" when there, and be themselves and "not someone else" including wearing a religious or intellectual mask. Prisoners and those working in prisons can see though masks quickly and the credibility of the Chaplain is compromised easily. If you are looking for a straightforward current treatment of the subject, there is enough material here to meet that need." — Dr. Michael Nace*

Part Ten

FAMILY PHOTOGRAPHS

Mark & Heather

Mark & Heather with Corban

Mark & Heather with Christian

APPENDIX

Article 1

Going Home from the Hospital, March 1995

I have visited two different hospitals several times this week. My friend Jason is on chemo therapy for Leukemia. Sue is on kidney dialysis and in critical condition after a heart attack. Michelle entered the ER early this morning with appendicitis and had surgery late this afternoon. Although a patient earlier this week, Jewell VanDyke is not in the hospital now — she went to her heavenly home early yesterday morning.

We all enjoy the prestige of having our own Dick VanDyke as a member and deacon of our church. Now we grieve with him and his family over the loss of his mother. Heaven is richer but we are greatly saddened. Just two days ago I visited Jewell. She looked weak but did not appear to be in critical condition. Yet she was gone in less than than twelve hours later. Dick is hurting. So are his brother and sister. They are feeling the pain of losing a loved one. I know how it feels. I remember my mom, her life and her death.

My mother's maiden name was Mabel L. Gladd. Her parents were born in Sweden. Mom only spoke Swedish until she moved to Warren (PA) during eighth grade. Then she had to learn English the hard but fast way!

Mom was very special. Most moms are special to their own children! After observing other moms, however, I believe mine was one of the best. Allow me the privilege of telling you about her.

Mom was a great cook. I truly enjoyed everything she made but especially her tuna and noodle casseroles. Swiss steak with potatoes and gravy, rabbit dinners and pumpkin pie.

Mom's public school cooking fame came to the attention of the Bethany Baptist Camp director in 1963. She was asked to work there and said "yes" to four tours of duty (1963-1966). She agreed with one simple condition! Bethany had to find something for her son to do. They were a hungry bunch and said that the 15 year old fellow would be welcome to wash dishes and mow grass! This sounded good to him because the camp was on Chautauqua Load which was known for great fishing.

What Mom could do with surplus food and limited budget was unbelievable. She would be up long before sunrise to make desserts and other treats. When young Missionary Don Trott had special dietary needs — Mom took good care of him. It was hard to keep the speakers, directors, missionaries, and other staff out of the kitchen — Mom always kept them full and laughing!

Almost every afternoon or early evening Mom could be seen looking for four-leaf clovers on the lawn next to the dinning hall. She usually found several on each hunt and would give them to campers of all ages. I still have a few she hand picked.

Mom was a single parent. *By now you may realize that it was just Mom and me during those years. She was a single parent before the title was vogue. If it were possible to interview her today for a single parent magazine — some would be shocked. Readers would learn that a person with character and a will to succeed can do so without being dependent on society. She went out and capitalized on what she could do and did it well. She made a living by cooking!*

Mom never used the word "entitlement." *She used words like "work" and "budget" and "stretch." We lived at 12 1/2 Canton Street until I went to college. Later she moved to 21 1/2 Elm Street. She never lived in a big place but she knew how to live within her income and still provide for her son.*

Mom was always reliable. *On Pennsylvania Avenue in Warren is a converted church facility. It is now a business called Reliable Furniture. Wouldn't it be nice, not to mention Biblical, if every church produced reliable people. Mom was such a person. She understood that her word was her honor.*

Mom's checkbook was not done by a calculator. *She did not have Quicken or Microsoft Money, yet her checks never bounced, her bills were never late, and her credit was never questioned.*

She wore the same blue magnetic earrings for as long as I can remember. Her favorite material seemed to be polyester and because she was quite tall she shopped by mail for coats and dresses. She wore some of them for years.

She owned three Volkswagens. In 1967, she bought her first new one which had a sticker price of under $1800. I am pretty sure she paid cash for it. She was one to save and then buy what she wanted.

Her love for sewing and crocheting provided many handmade gifts bearing the "Made by Mabel" label. I have one such coat from 1970's that has "shrunk" over the years and doesn't fit well any more. Yet there will always be room for it in my closet to remind me of her labor of love.

•

Mom had a great sense of humor. She was always telling jokes and pulling little pranks on folks. Two immediately come to mind. It seems that the camp bell came up missing during one week when Reverend Alvin Ross was director and Dr. David Nettleton was the speaker. Reverend Ross lined up all the campers and staff on the ball diamond and threaten that there would be no dinner until someone confessed and the bell returned. This scene went on for what seemed like hours. No one moved. Finally, the word was leaked that the director should check his room. Sure enough — there it was. It was a long time later that Mom told me that she and Dr. Nettleton moved it by themselves! Doc and I laughed over it one last time when he spoke at a Bible Conference in Johnson City some years ago just before his home-going.

Another laugh involved Dr. Duane Brown who had planned a prank on his campers one night. He and Mom privately set up a toast of juice spiked with alum spice (produces immediate pucker power). Of course he was to be spared but not with Mom in the picture. I believe Sandy (Eggleston) Hine helped her switch the glasses. When Dr. Brown toasted something important and said, "Bottoms up" he got the surprise fo his life. He just about turned inside out! Mom enjoyed every minute of it.

Mom was a great friend. Mom knew how much I loved to hunt. I remember the year she bought a hunting license and took me to a farm and walked through the fields with me. As it was to be... she kicked out the only rabbit we saw that day. She pointed the .22 rifle at it and said, "There it goes, there it goes!" She never fired a shot but gave me a hunting memory that is still vivid today.

Mom had a great hope. One of the certainties of life is death. A throat difficulty in the spring of 1983 turned out to be cancer. A few months later the Lord decided that it was time for Mom to go home from the hospital. She left Warren General and arrived in heaven on the last day of 1983 on earth but the first day of eternity for Mom.

A few days later (following my pastoral tradition) I stayed behind in the funeral home when others left. I watched the director lower the platform inside the casket to its lowest position. I watched as he carefully tucked the lining material and gently closed the casket. Then I walked with them to the hearse and drove to the cemetery where I watched them lower the casket into the vault, seal it, and begin to fill in the grave. It was a very cold January day in Pennsylvania.

The Bible, however, tells me that it was a beautiful day in heaven. The temperature was perfect. Everywhere Mom looked she saw the glory of the Lord. She was then able to see perfectly without her glasses. She looked around and realized that there were no hospitals, no sickness, no pain, no radiation or chemotherapy, no crippling diseases, no heartaches, no loneliness, and no more tears.

I imagine it wasn't long before she was greeted by the Lord and personally welcomed to her new home. I'm sure heaven was ready for Mom because she was prepared for heaven by her personal faith in Christ. She was a believer, unique servant of the Lord, and a tremendous mother.

I also believe a familiar and kind voice soon caught her attention. "Hello, Mabel," came the greeting from Pastor Ernest Hook. "It's good to see you." He stood tall — totally without the signs of his crippling earthly disease he had the first time he entered our home thirty years earlier and invited us to work at Bethany.

What a tremendous impact Bethany had on Mom's life and certainly mine. Pastors with names like… Ross, Robb, Margesson, Brown, Thompson, Fuller, Eggleston, Felt… missionaries like Trott, Blood, and Armstrong she called her friends. One college president even became her accomplice in camp crime!

As I walked out of the hospital today, I thought of the many individuals who have gone home from there. Some have gone to their residences here on earth. Many, though, like Mom and Jewell, have left directly for their new home in heaven.

I realized, as I headed up Interstate 81 to Richland that some day I very well may take the journey to my heavenly home from the hospital. So be it.

What a reunion it will be. First of all I want to see Jesus but then I'm going to start looking for that tall smiling lady called Mabel by her friends but I called her Mom.

I'm thankful Mom didn't leave me behind when she went to work at Bethany because it was there that the Lord saved me that very first summer.

I'm thankful Mom didn't live on "entitlements" because I learned valuable lessons about hard work and careful living.

I'm thankful Mom didn't mind hunting because I learned how much she loved me when I saw her kicking brush piles and walking in the fields.

I'm thankful Mom didn't lose her sense of humor when faced with difficulty because looking at the lighter side and having a good laugh has often put thinks back into perspective for me.

I'm thankful Mom didn't say "no" to returning to Bethany year after year because the Lord used the ministry of God's Word in that place more than any other to call me into the ministry.

I'm thankful Mom did so much for me! Going home from the hospital Mom entered into that reward for those who know the Lord and faithfully live for Him. Mom certainly had much reward waiting for her. God is good to give us good mothers!

Article 2

Rifles, Respect & Reward, 1993

I remember the first rifle I bought when I was eight years old. That Sheridan 5mm air rifle is still in the gun cabinet. It brings back many memories of my Pennsylvania home.

I devoted many hours of my childhood as an imaginary Cavalry officer carrying that single shot rifle. During recreation of WWII drama the Sheridan often became a Springfield '03A3, a M1 or B.A.R. — plastic enemies fell off snow banks or dirt piles with great regularity! Feathered friends and rabbits were protected from their natural prey (neighborhood cats) by my Sheridan, my constant companion for many years.

My greatest memory associated with the Sheridan, however, is that work has its rewards. You see Dad did not buy me the rifle. He offered me work and I earned it. Dad had a work contract with the United Refinery in my hometown to repair and recondition their petroleum pumps – the kind you see out on the farm, in factories or on construction sites. These hand pumps had to be maintained on a regular basis.

So Dad made me an offer. He would pay me most of his earnings if I wanted to recondition the pumps. He then offered me a contract. I accepted. Then I made a want list; on the top was a Sheridan. He taught me the value of work at an early age. He taught me that what I wanted to earn and what I wanted to have was up to me.

It took me about 45 minutes to dismantle, recondition, and reassemble each pump. Dad paid me $3.00 each. Wow, $3.00 in less than an hour back in 1955; big bucks for an eight year old. Did I work fast? Yes sir! But was that my only objective? No!

At the age of eight I learned that quality is the most important aspect of any work. More than once a pump did not pass Dad's inspection. I would have to do it over again. Sure I wanted to make as much money as possible, but my father's approval meant more to me than monetary gain.

Yes, I did earn the Sheridan. Matter of fact, I not only earned the price of the rifle, but I also bought a special sight for it, and a war's supply of ammo (2500) from the earnings made on one Saturday afternoon in my father's garage.

I wonder what memories we are creating for our children. Do they know the value of work? Do they have memories associated with their possessions?

Society is rampant with those who believe the government owes them a living; that the President is father and he should be taking care of us. As my son would say, "NOT!" We are to provide for ourselves and our own families; if we do not, well, we are worse than infidels.

Walking by the gun cabinet is a walk down memory lane. It reminds me of a tremendous lesson. From generation to generation we are to teach our children that work honors the Lord. You see beside the Sheridan in another cabinet slot is an Ithaca M37. It is my son Mark's shotgun. Did I buy it for him? No! Did he work for it? Yes. Many hours were spent at a local farm with a shovel, but he knows he earned that Ithaca. There was much more value for Mark in learning to work than there was in the price of the shotgun.

What are we teaching our children? I suggest that we teach them that possessions are a privilege not a right; that honest hard work has its reward; that quality is more important than quantity; that employer approval is more important than affluence; and that in the biggest picture: work is not ultimately about wages.

Fatherhood has its responsibilities as well as privileges. As fathers we are to transfer to our children the work ethic that God established and Americans have demonstrated for years. God has recorded for us the proper work ethic: He worked and then rested. His comment each day was that His work, His creation, was good; then He rested. Work has its reward.

Father's Day honor is only deserved if we are a model of hard and good work. I'm thankful for a great lesson Dad taught me back in 1955.

Article 3

Memorial Day, 2006

Veterans, I am proud to know you and serve beside you; because you are willing to fight for peace! When I see you and thousands like you... in BDUs, DCUs and our new ACUs, well, I am proud to serve with you.

I look into your faces and see...

Men and women who have served with distinction in the smoke and debris of the World Trade Center, in the mountains of Afghanistan, and in the hot desert of Iraq.

I see... men and woman who have brought honor to family and friends.

I see... men and woman who place commitment over comfort and convenience.

I see... men and woman who honor the flag over fame and fortune.

I see... men and woman who understand that freedom is not free.

The United States of America has three patriotic holidays.

On the fourth of July we celebrate the birth of our nation. We mark this birthday by parades, ceremonies, family picnics, and beautiful fireworks.

On Veterans' Day we honor all men and women who have worn the uniforms of the United States Military. We have more parades and ceremonies.

Memorial Day is a national day of remembrance, reflection and reverence.

Memorial Day is best understood by visualizing an elderly, silver haired woman standing by the mantel of her fireplace looking at the picture of a young soldier during WW 2. He was her father who never returned to his young daughter. He was a soldier killed on the bloody beaches of Normandy.

Memorial Day is best understood by visualizing an aging woman looking at the dog-eared photograph of her husband and father of her now adult children posing beside his Huey "Chopper" just before his final and fatal mission. He was an aviator who died in the steaming rice paddies of Vietnam.

Memorial Day is best understood by visualizing a father and mother dreaming about their daughter, a pilot who will never give them grandchildren because she was killed in the rugged mountains of Afghanistan.

Memorial Day is best understood by visualizing a young boy in a baseball uniform gazing at a digital photograph of his father who will never play ball with his son because he was a Marine killed in the hot desert of Iraq.

Memorial Day is perpetually understood by viewing rows of white crosses and stars of David on green fields of national cemeteries both in American in Europe.

First Time Experience — This year, for the first time, thousands of American families will truly and emotionally recognize this national holiday.

From California to Maine, many traditional family gatherings will have one less table setting. The absent family member's military service ended in death.

With continuing American casualties in Afghanistan and Iraq, Memorial Day places a more intense spotlight on lost life and grieving families. Photo albums stir memories. Sacrifice now has a face — a known face.

Respect or Disrespect — I witnessed many memorial ceremonies in Iraq for fallen soldiers. Standing in the hot sun I thought of the families in the United States who would now more greatly and personally respect the intended purpose of Memorial Day.

We often insulate ourselves from the pain of others until we experience it ourselves. Empathy quickly replaces apathy when the grave marker has our family name on it.

Price of Freedom — Our country sets asides Memorial Day as a national holiday, a "Holy Day" to remember and respect military personnel who have died to provide and preserve the liberties we enjoy.

Americans seemingly value less what costs little. Value increases when we or our loved ones personally pay the price.

A Spiritual Analogy

For millions of Americans the price of eternal salvation is equally undervalued. Respect and reverence are lost without understanding the personal sacrifice of the Lord Jesus Christ at Calvary.

Presidents and Jesus Christ

As a teenager I visited Virginia and our nation's capitol for the first time. I saw Mount Vernon where our first president lived and the small room across from Ford Theatre where our 16th president died. I believed they lived and died as history records.

For many years I pretty much believed in Jesus Christ the same way. He was a historical character who lived and died; nothing personal about it for me.

However, this all changed in 1963 when a preacher explained the gospel to me. He said, "God loves you but your sin separates you from Him. Therefore, God sent his Son and He, Jesus, died for your sin on Calvary."

Forgiveness is offered to all those who believe that Jesus died for them. I knew this mentally from years of Sunday school but I was still uncertain.

Family Name on the Marker

I did not understand and did not value the death of Christ until I learned two facts from the Word of God.

First, I am a sinner and sin destroys freedom. "For all have sinned and come short of the glory of God" (Romans 3:10).

Second, Christ died for my sin so that I might have eternal life. "For God so loved the world that He gave His only begotten son that whosoever believes in Him should not perish but have everlasting life" (John 3:16).

The preacher told me to read this verse and substitute my name in each appropriate place. He told me to read this repeatedly until I could see myself in the verse.

I read it like this... "For God so loved Doug that He gave His only begotten son that [if] Doug [will] believe in Him, Doug [will] not perish but Doug [will] have everlasting life" (John 3:16).

Finally, I saw that although the Cross of Calvary was where Christ died for me, in my place. Calvary marks the place where God simultaneously demonstrated His hatred of sin and His love for me.

I have never looked at Calvary quite the same way again. I realized that day July 18, 1963, that the symbol of the cross is God's way of memorializing His Son who died that we might have forgiveness and freedom from sin.

Spiritual Memorial Day

Today we remember those men and women in uniform who died that we might live in freedom. We honor them today for all they gave us by their ultimate sacrifice. We do not doubt nor disrespect their sacrifice upon our behalf. We appreciate them and our freedom.

In a similar way, shouldn't we honor the Lord Jesus Christ Who died that we might live? If we don't, perhaps it is because we have not looked long enough to see ourselves as needing forgiveness from sin. Perhaps we don't see ourselves as sinful.

Look today to Calvary. See Christ taking your place. Read John 3:16 until you understand.

Article 4

My Father and Friend, 1995
Written to Celebrate Dad's Eightieth Birthday

I am a very fortunate person. God has blessed me with a great wife, tremendous children, super friends and an excellent church family. I anticipate each and every day because something good is always happening!

When I think of all the people I have known in my lifetime, the most influential human being in my life has been my father and friend, Robert Ferry.

Dad was born on January 11, 1915. This month he will celebrate his 80th birthday. He lived most of his life in Warren County in the great state of Pennsylvania. However, Dad and Gladys (my stepmother and very special lady) moved to Pulaski in 1993 when their health began to slip. I have tremendously enjoyed having them live nearby during these past two years.

Yet my memory was jogged recently when Dad drove by me in his Nissan truck. I had a flashback that sent chills throughout my whole body. I vividly remembered an earlier and similar view of Dad through a car window when I was about 15 and divorce had separated us. I can still see him driving by in his 1962 International Scout. Our relationship was almost wrecked by the tragedy of divorce.

Early in my life we were inseparable. My earliest memories are of happy times with beagles chasing rabbits and busting woodchucks at unbelievable distances. We fished and hunted together. We loaded ammunition together and dreamed about great deer or elk hunts we would take together.

But divorce took Dad and me through a three year separation that has permanently affected me. We lived apart from October of 1962 to September 1965. By my choice I saw Dad only a few times during those three years.

I did see him for a few moments on the first day of deer season in 1964. I had just let several deer pass in snow covered apple trees because I could not see any antlers — although I was sure the last one was a buck. Within moments a rifle shot confirmed my thoughts. I started down the hill and waved at the lucky hunter. When I was almost to him I realized the hunter was Dad. We exchanged a few casual remarks about the real nice nine-point buck and then I left him there. It's one hunting memory that still haunts me. I left my Dad out there alone to drag the deer out of the woods. Whenever that event is recalled I always have a heavy sense of unbearable remorse!

I remember that Dad did take me to college — but we were very distant. Early that first year a Godly professor wisely counseled me toward reconciliation with Dad. I remember that visit in September in the Scout on a dirt road called Brown Run; years earlier Dad had taken me fishing there and taught me how to drive the '46 Willy Jeep. We parked just past where the spring water always flows out of the hillside. It was there in the Allegheny Mountains where we talked and talked and became friends again. Dad was always my father but for a while we weren't friends.

That event happened almost 30 years ago. Dad has been my father and friend ever since. The clouds that entered my life passed and the sun was shining again. We began to rebuild our relationship into one of joy, fulfillment and utmost intimacy.

I now know that the greatest joys come out of the deepest sorrows, much like how flowers look the most beautiful when set against the darker backgrounds of earth. Perhaps it is just that we appreciate the very most those things which we almost lose. We often do not fully understand how precious some folks are until they are gone forever. I am thankful for my second opportunity to enjoy my father and friend.

And I do love Dad. He has a generous heart and given me so much. I cherish the days we have had together as father and son. We have had lots of experiences together in Pennsylvania, Canada, Michigan, Vermont, Massachusetts, Wyoming, Texas, Ohio, and New York.

Dad was there to teach me how to operate the lathe, mills, drill presses; to sharpen drills; to read blueprints, micrometers, dial calipers; to analyze, think and create; and to give an honest day's work for a day's pay.

Dad was there to teach me how to load ammunition, breathe properly and squeeze the trigger; to dismantle and assemble an assortment of firearms; and to hunt safely.

Dad was there to explain how to build the best way just about anything you can imagine. He designed machines that always bore the unmistakable imprint of his creative mind, the endless pursuit of detail, and the relentless desire for excellence. He used stainless steel, aluminum, cadmium platted nuts and bolts and finished most assembled units in forest green! They were not just machines but the work of an artist!

Dad has been there for almost every meaningful event that I can remember.

Dad was there to teach me how to repair pumps and earn the value of work in 1955.

Dad was there when I shot eight or was it 11 woodchucks without missing in 1956 (an on going debate)!

Dad was there when I missed my first buck in 1959.

Dad was there to bring me home from jail in 1964.

Dad was there when I had cancer surgery in 1966.

Dad was there to build a tree stand that same year for me to use during what some thought would be my last deer season.

Dad was there fishing with me in Canada in 1967.

Dad was there when I married Theresa in 1968.

Dad was there in Wyoming in 1970 to show me how to shoot antelope at 400 plus yards.

Dad was there when I graduated from college in 1973.

Dad was there in 1974 to pull the ticks off me in Texas during a most unusual deer hunt!

Dad was there when my kids wanted a tree house in Vermont in 1976.

Dad was there when we shot elk in Wyoming in 1977.

Dad was there when I lived in Mesquite, Texas and was attending Dallas Seminary in 1982.

Dad was there to help finish the dormer on our home in Fonda, New York in 1988.

Dad was there to see Mark marry Heather in 1994.

Dad has been around almost 80 years now. He has been and he still is a very special person. Dad loves to tell stories. Some of them are thread bare but I like to hear him tell them over and over again. By listening to him I can walk along side him during his childhood. I can relive with him some of the good and bad times. I am thankful for Dad's sharp mind and great sense of humor. We can laugh together and remember together.

I treasure the days that God grants to us now. We can never replace those lost years, but I thank God for Bethany Baptist Camp where God gave me the title of son in 1963. It was at Bethany where I became a part of the family of God. I am certainly thankful for my Heavenly Father. But I also want to thank God for Dr. Jack Jacobs who gave me guidance in restoring my broken relationship with my earthly father.

Birthdays are special and we honor those who are another year older. Although most people arrive at the event because they just keep eating and avoid playing in traffic — not Dad. Everyday is an adventure for him. Dad tackles every job with anticipation and the attitude that he can do just about anything and do it right.

I have watched him for many years now and that is the conclusion I have made. Dad can do just about anything he puts his mind to do. What a privilege it has been to know him, learn from him, hunt with him, dream with him, and share life with him.

Birthdays are times to mark accomplishment. I want to mark his 80th birthday with great appreciation for his example, his life, and his love. I am thankful for my great heritage. I am proud to be his son. Without reservation, I can say I am proud of my father and friend, Robert Ferry.

Article 5

Key for College Success, 1993

College is an investment. This fall you will begin to invest time and money in preparation for your future. Your return on investment greatly depends on how well you succeed in college. The following concept may help you. You might learn by instruction or logic how to use a scheduling procedure, but I failed to learn this until I had messed up several semesters of college. Forgotten exams and assignments (i.e., books to read, papers to write, extra credit opportunities, etc.) constantly hurt me. If you already know how to do this, great; otherwise, read on, my friend!

INTRODUCTION

*During the first class of each course you will receive a syllabus which will list all course objectives, requirements, tests, grading scales, calendar of events, etc. This important paper will become the basis of your plan. (Usually the first day or two students refer to being in the state of **"Syllabus Shock"** because of all they will be required to do in the following 15 weeks.)*

*YOU NEED A SYLLABUS FOR **EVERY** COURSE - DON'T LEAVE CLASS WITHOUT ONE!*

STEP #1   YOUR APPOINTMENT CALENDAR

*After you have gathered all your syllabi (Latin: syllabus is singular; syllabi are plural.), get a good large academic calendar (11" X 17" open). Block out one night or early Saturday morning to **CALENDAR** your semester's work. This is the **Key for College Success**. You need to do this before your second day of any class! Don't skip this -- get it done. Also take a copy of your class schedule and tape it on the inside front cover of your calendar for quick reference. After two to three weeks you will know it by memory, but until then keep it in your calendar.*

SPECIAL NOTE: BLOCK IN SUNDAY FOR WORSHIP AND WEDNESDAY FOR PRAYER MTG.—PLAN FOR IT.

STEP #2   YOUR TESTS

With syllabi and calendar before you, begin with your first course syllabus and record the tests on the dates when the exams will be given. Record every quiz, test, exam, mid-term, and final—all of them. Then go to the next course syllabus and do likewise. Continue with each syllabus until ALL known tests are recorded on your calendar. You will never be surprised about an exam—seems good already, doesn't it?

STEP #3   YOUR WRITING ASSIGNMENTS

Start over again with the first syllabus and record all the writing assignments on the dates that they are to be completed. Some of these will be assignments which can be done easily in one night. Great! Do it the night before or earlier (more on this later). Okay, go ahead and go through all the syllabi and record all the assignments on the dates due. Well, did any of them fall on the same day; several, right? Seems that all professors think they are the only teachers around when establishing requirements. Here is where this **Key for College Success** is going to start paying off. When two or more assignments are due on the same day, even if they require only one night's work (3-5 hours), you will not be able to do two or more without losing some sleep or else quality. Sleep is rather important—especially when trying to stay awake in class the next day or on a date (I am realistic)! Quality is important if you want to graduate—right? So when assignments start to pile up, you have to look BACKWARD on your calendar for a FREE night or Saturday when you can do the written assignments. It may take more than one block of time; if so; look backward for it on your calendar.

STEP #4   YOUR READING ASSIGNMENTS

So far you have on your calendar the upcoming TESTS and WRITTEN ASSIGNMENTS. Now as you start through your syllabi for the third time, you will be scheduling all your READING assignments. Write down when they are due. I mean both your textbook and collateral reading. Listen closely: most of the time you will find your reading to be worth 10% to 30% of your FINAL GRADE. Did that impress you? It should have. Reading makes the difference between A's and B's, B's and C's and often C's and D's. Do I have to say more? Reading is simple, but you have to allow time for it. You cannot read a 300 page book in two or three hours, but it can be read easily in six settings of an hour each at 50 pages per hour. If you cannot read that fast, allow more time. Remember now, you have to read PRIOR to that date. So look BACKWARD on your calendar for free evenings or Saturdays or days when you have no classes and schedule 50 pages per hour of a specific book. Do this backward until the total number of pages is scheduled. Remember that this reading is just as important as any class to attend, test to be taken or written project to be completed. Don't skip it! Do this *for EVERY reading assignment you have. CALENDAR THEM ALL; account for every page.*

STEP #5   *YOUR EXTRA CREDIT OPPORTUNITIES*

Now you have all TESTS, WRITING, and READING assignments on your calendar; starting to look full, isn't it? But NOW you know WHAT you have to do for the semester and WHEN you are going to do each task. Feels good, doesn't it? What is left? Well, sometimes professors will give extra credit assignments—do you have time? Well now, look at your calendar and see. Do you? You now know what you have to do, when you are going to do it, and what else you CAN do. Schedule the extra work WHEN and WHERE you have the time.

STEP #6   *YOUR SOCIAL LIFE*

Anything else? Yes, such a thing as social life does have a part in your college experience! Social matters like dating should NOT be put on the schedule until you know WHEN and IF you have the time. You are at college to gain an education—right? I hope so. However, grant yourself some leisure time on your calendar. Schedule sports and cultural events, but stay in control to achieve your ultimate goal: an education and graduation.

STEP #7   *YOUR TEMPTATION*

You may sometimes or often be tempted to cut class but just consider the following: You and/or your parents are paying a tremendous price for your education; probably over $20,000 per year. You will be taking about 30 credit hours the first year. So, 15 hours per week times 15 weeks is 225 class hours per semester or 450 per year. Divide that into $20,000 and you will find that each class hour costs over $44.00. Remember this when thinking about cutting class. You lose both financially and educationally. By the way, guaranteed, one of three things will happen whenever you cut: 1) the professor will have the BEST lecture of the semester, 2) an unannounced test will be given, or 3) someone will have a party! Don't skip classes.

CONCLUSION
 ➣ *Make your schedule and then live by your schedule.*
 ➣ *Personal discipline will make the difference between success and failure.*
 ➣ *Never go to bed until your day's work is done.*
 ➣ *Don't be sidetracked; stay on the main course.*
 ➣ *Enjoy your success and praise the Lord.*

Article 6

Where Did the Time Go?, 1995

I remember the evening in 1990 that our daughter Julaine, a high school junior at the time, asked if she could apply to Baptist Bible College for the next fall and skip her senior year.

A war was on the horizon in Kuwait and as a chaplain in the New York Army National Guard I had just been ordered to the sand box. With an uncertain future, Julaine checked out what courses she needed and I called to see what BBC would think about the idea.

Julaine never considered attending any other school. Her objective was clear: she wanted to prepare to serve the Lord. She decided that BBC, the ministry school, was her only choice. Mom and I approved completely!

Julaine left for BBC in August of 1991. By taking a heavy course load plus summer school, Julaine was the only Pulaski senior with 41 college credits completed when she graduated in June of 1992.

Although I never went to the gulf, that military build up and God's sovereign hand moved Julaine to BBC one year earlier than expected.

That seems like only a few weeks ago. But then the trip to Butterworth Hospital in Grand Rapids seems like only a few months ago. Julaine was born one week after I graduated from Cornerstone College. Our Sunday School teacher announced that Julaine was the most beautiful baby he had ever seen. He lost points that day with some other parents but we thought he was absolutely right!

Julaine was two when we entered our first pastorate. She was four when she accepted Christ as her Savior. She was seven when she drove her brother's go-cart through the church's basement window! She was ten when we went camping together in Texas. She was 15 when she placed first in the Leaders In Training program at Camp of the Nations and began her camp counseling ministry.

Julaine is a reminder that years pass quickly. I can remember our father and daughter dates, camping trips, basketball games, cross country meets, and visits going here and there.

I had mixed emotions when Julaine left for BBC. I was filled with pride yet felt empty that she was leaving our home. I was thrilled about her wise choices in high school and confident about her adult decisions yet I have missed her day by day conversations and questions.

I remember listening to her excitement about classes at BBC. She has experienced tremendous spiritual growth. Both veterans and new professors have taught her much and been a blessing. When she graduates this week I will probably ask myself again, "Where did the time go?"

May 18 is the date that reminds us to celebrate the gift that the Lord gave Theresa and me in 1973. Julaine has been a tremendous blessing during these past 22 years.

Thanks are due to Baptist Bible College faculty and staff for ministering to our daughter. The productivity of their service is seen in her life; for helping her to develop her mind, tenderize her heart, and expand her horizons.

Where did the time go? It has not been lost, but it has been invested in all that Julaine has become. Theresa and I have our memories as a rich treasure. We can remember and rejoice, because we have no greater joy than to know that our children walk in truth.

Article 7

Father's Day Criteria, 1998
(Adapted from Titus 1:5-9)

A father must be blameless as a manager of his children for God.

A father must not be arrogant but sensitive in leading his children to make good decisions, not forcing on them his own ideas and opinions.

A father must not be quickly angered but one who controls his own spirit and thus one who demonstrates the fruitfulness of the Spirit filled life before his children.

A father must not be bonded to booze but one who spends long periods of time with Christ so that it is evident to his children that Christ is the greatest influence in his life.

A father must not be quarrelsome but tender and compassionate toward his children so that they might see the love and patience of God through him.

A father must not be a lover of money but one who finds contentment in God's provisions so that his children might learn to appreciate eternal values more than temporal pleasures.

A father must be hospitable and enjoy opening his home and heart to his children's friends so that they will be attracted rather than repelled by his attitudes and beliefs.

A father must be a lover of what is good in his children and offer gentle correction of their faults so that virtue is cultivated and error is diminished.

A father must be in control of himself so that his children know that this fruit of the Spirit is present in his life.

A father must be just so that his children can understand right from wrong by his personal lifestyle.

A father must be holy so that his children can see and follow his love for Christ and his hatred of sin.

A father must be able to control his sexual desires so that his children can respect him and have a model of purity to follow into adulthood.

A father must hold tightly to the faithful word so that he may be able, by healthy teaching, to encourage proper behavior and correct improper behavior in his children.

Article 8

Making Lumber Out of Logs, 1994

Several years ago a group of New England pastors met to discuss the state of the GARBC. I was present at the meeting. As the talk turned to Baptist Bible College -- much criticism was leveled at the advertisements using sports to attract students, the changes in curriculum, etc. Several made statements that the graduates were just not the caliber of years gone by. Then a pastor from Maine spoke up with this remark, "The lumber coming out of the saw mill will be only as good as the logs we send in." I'll never forget that comment.

This Saturday morning a fine young man from our church is graduating from Practical Bible College. He was a good log when he went to PBC and he is now coming out a pretty fine piece of lumber to be used by the Lord in the building of His kingdom. The PBC faculty has prepared him well. This week he accepted a call to pastor a small Baptist church here in New York. I remember his first visit to Calvary; his faithfulness; his eagerness to learn and grow. I remember our close relationship and the opportunity to mentor my young friend. He was good quality going to PBC -- he had the stuff the Lord requires. But it was also a good faculty that sharpened his skills; challenged his commitment; and stretched his horizons.

My son, Mark, is graduating tomorrow from Baptist Bible College. He entered BBC just four years ago. What a change God has made in my son. I think he was a pretty good guy going in, but how significantly the faculty of BBC has shaped him into a tremendous blessing.

During a recent trip home I asked Mark which faculty member made the greatest contribution to his life. It was a joy to hear how several faculty members have truly been used of the Lord in his life. He mentioned Gary Hauck, Jim Lytle, Joseph Schloegel, Dennis Wilhite, Dan Hayden, and a newcomer, Don Holdridge, with great appreciation.

I should probably mention that Mark entered BBC with a desire to be a commercial pilot. He was at BBC primarily because I insisted he complete an associates degree before entering flight school. At the end of his first year he called to ask if he could transfer into the Youth Ministries Major! It has been steady growth since.

*I believe **Dr. Hauck** made the first impact on Mark. His creative ways of teaching the Old Testament courses truly impressed Mark. Involving Mark in some of the classroom drama really motivated him to dig deeper into the Word. Mark may have picked up from Dr. Hauck the quotation he has in his Bible, "It is a sin to bore people with the Word of God." Thanks, Gary, for working in the mill. You would be proud of Mark's ability to creatively teach precious Biblical truth.*

***Dr. Lytle** presented Mark with two invaluable gifts: a DayTimer and an excellent interpretive methodology. You will never see Mark without his DayTimer. He is on schedule and knows what he is doing by the day and by the hour! The lessons learned in Building a Biblical Lifestyle and his course in hermeneutics are heard in every sermon. Mark's senior sermons were prime examples of insightful observation, solid interpretation, appropriate correlation, and excellent application; learned well from a capable teacher. Thanks, Jim, for working in the mill. You would be proud of Mark's ability to rightly open the Word and communicate its eternal truth.*

***Mr. Schloegel** taught Mark theology. I remember one visit home when Mark came into the living room, opened his DayTimer and started down a list of seven or eight questions he had from theology class. They were significant questions that had Mark thinking. He wanted to run them by dad, sure; but Mr. Schloegel brought Mark into the World of theology. Concepts that challenged his understanding, pushed him to form his own theological views -- not just accept hand-me-down doctrine. Mark now has a good grasp of systematic theology. Thanks, Joe, for working in the mill. You would be proud of Mark's ability to think Biblically and fit his understanding of the Word into systematic and theological harmony.*

***Mr. Dennis Wilhite** made several contributions to Mark's education, but by far what has been learned is the value of discipleship or personal mentoring. Mr. Wilhite has also enlarged Mark's use of his DayTimer! Mark now has pictures of his youth group arranged neatly with birthdays, vocational goals, prayer requests, hobbies, etc. Mr. Wilhite, most importantly, has given Mark ministry perspective. What you build into people by personal involvement is what is most important. Discipleship is not a six week course but two people on an adventure together to discover God. Thanks, Dennis, for working in the mill. You would be proud of Mark's DayTimer and his concern for and involvement with young people.*

***Mr. Dan Hayden** has helped Mark learn how to take off, fly and land a sermon! Building on interpretive skills, good theology, creative teaching,* *and a love for people; Mr. Hayden has polished Mark's communication skills in the pulpit. He has also given Mark a love for the pastoral epistles that makes his preaching vibrant. Thanks, Dan, for working in the mill. You would be proud of Mark's ability to rightly open the Word and effectively communicate.*

Dr. Don Holdridge *has shown Mark how important personal contact is in ministry. Mark tells me that Dr. Holdridge attends just about every function including all chapels, is available at all times, and is seen everywhere at all times. It is obvious to Mark that Dr. Holdridge cares about students. Thanks, Don, for working in the mill. You would be proud of Mark's concern for people, the willingness to go the extra mile to be there for folks.*

I believe that churches and pastors must send BBC good logs. That is our responsibility. I am writing this, however, to say that there are some good laborers in the mill investing their lives in another generation of servants. Tomorrow when Mark receives his degree I will be personally elated, but also cognizant that I am indebted to all of you who have been working in the mill to produce the lumber. Thanks, men, for cutting, shaping, and sanding my son. The Lord now has a fine piece of wood to use.

May the Lord continue to grant you grace and wisdom in your ministry.

Article 9

It's time...

[Written by author on the occasion of the marriage his son, Mark]
September 1994

"It's time..." my wife Theresa said about six a.m. on January 9th, 1971. Off we went to the Newfane Community Hospital (NY) to await the arrival of our son. Later that day Mark Ernest became a member of our family. His time with us since has been a tremendous blessing.

"It's time..." Mark would tell me when the five minutes were up and it was time for another blast from the Bianca breath freshener. Each blast would buy five minutes of silence from the four year old so that the preacher could continue uninterrupted. This routine would begin at the hour the pastor was to finish. Mark would quietly nudge me every five minutes after eyeing my wristwatch continuously. The Bianca blast worked perfectly.

"It's time..." four and a half year old Mark would say as we headed for the sand dunes on the edge of Grandville (MI). He was always anxious to go with me. It was there that Mark shot my S&W .22 for the first time. With a little help the young fellow hit the 55 gallon drum five out of six shots at about 90 yards.

"It's time... to build a tree house," five year old Mark told Theresa and me in East Wallingford (VT). We had a problem, though, we had no trees in our yard. We looked over the situation and saw that a large stump might be our alternative. So Grandpa Ferry lovingly engineered the house that he transported to our home from Pennsylvania. It was assembled and painted and Mark enjoyed probably the finest stump-house in all Vermont. It was in that stump house where six year old Mark said, "It's time... to trust Christ as my Savior."

"It's time... to go," eight year old Mark said as we loaded the Honda CT-90 with our tent and rain gear; another Friday night camping in the Berkshire Hills (MA). We had long conversations about a small boy's thoughts and dreams inside that tent. We were not much for cooking, so Mark would remind me early on Saturday, "It's time... for breakfast at McDonald's." Another great overnight with Mark concluded with his favorites: pancakes and hot chocolate.

"It's time... to feed the pigeons," said 14 year old Mark. Our garage in Fonda (NY) was home at one point for over 40 feathered friends. A messy hobby but far better than the habits of drugs or drinking!

"It's time... to break the school record," Mark said as we went to New York state qualifiers. His ability in the 400 meter hurtles was awesome. I watched with deep pride as he did the fastest time of his career: 56.7 seconds. Although it was the night of a father and son banquet at Calvary Baptist in Richland, we were in Baldwinsville where 19 year old Mark set the fastest recorded time for the event in the history of Pulaski.

"It's time... to stop dating and think about courting," 19 year old Mark told Theresa and me. Dr. Douglas Combs trained the counselors at Lamoka Camp (NY) in 1990 and had a super impact on Mark. His mind was made up -- he was going to hold out for the right young lady and then begin courting.

"It's time... for my boys to go home on Saturday and it hurts me to see them leave camp," said Mark as we watched and listened to this 19 year old explain the difficulties of their home life, spiritual struggles, fighting churches, hypocritical parents, etc. With tears in his eyes and a choked voice he related to us the heartaches of the young fellows under his care for just six days. Mark's favorite object lesson for cabin devo's was the use of a chem light to demonstrate that we need to see Christ broken on the cross for our sin before we can understand and see the light of the gospel. Also we need to be broken before the light of the gospel can shine through us! God has been developing a pastor's heart in our son.

"It's time... to start courting, " Mark said enthusiastically to us on the phone. "Who's the young lady," we asked our almost 20 year old son? "You remember that sharp girl I pointed out at Camp Lamoka last summer? Her name is Heather Allgrim. She visited BBC this week and we talked for hours. We have agreed to write and see each other." We did remember the slender, polite, and attractive young lady named Heather. We had talked about her mission's trip to Utah and our mutual friends. She was a delight and we were immediately thankful for the Lord's direction in their courting.

"It's time... to choose a major," our 21 year old son told us. "Is it okay to transfer into the four year Youth Ministries major?" Theresa and I were elated! The Lord was answering prayer and giving Mark a call into the ministry.

"It's time... to consider a summer internship," our 22 year old son told us. Before long a call came from Batavia (NY) to spend the summer working with their youth. It was a tremendous summer. Pastor Shirk gave a great report on our son. He told us, "Mark has a sensitive heart for young people, a good knowledge of the Word, and he has the seeds of being a great preacher. You can be proud of him." And proud of our son we are!

"It's time... to give her the ring," Theresa and I learned over the phone from Mark. The song he wrote, the video, the timing -- all were thought out and prepared. It was time and the delightful young lady from Hornell said, "yes," to the tall, thin young man from Richland.

[The following lines are adapted from his proposal song, "I love you, I do, I do!"]

"It's time..." now for Heather to reach out for Mark's hand to share all that a lifetime can bring. You two can do anything if it's done in the power of His name.

"It's time..." for your two hearts that are beating in time and with true music playing in your mind; for your two dreams to become one and begin the one race to run.

"It's time..." for you to say, "I love you, I do, I do!"

"It's time..." for Mark and Heather to begin their life together. Theresa and I know they will honor the Lord and receive His blessing. We anticipate the impact they will have on young lives in the church and community where the Lord leads them. So now we thank our Lord that "It's time" in His divine plan to see our son, Mark, join in holy marriage with this fine young lady, Heather. We know God will bless their home and ministry because they have both placed Him first in their lives.

We are blessed. "It's time... now to rejoice!" For we have no greater joy than to know that our children walk in truth.

We love you, Mark & Heather
May God richly bless you.

Article 10

Dresses, Daughters & Decency, 1994

Folks do not know me as the best dressed pastor in northern New York. More than once my ties have been the target for pointed humor. For all self respect to be salvaged —I have relied on my wife to pick out tasteful ties for several years. More recently I have had the help of my son and daughter!

Four years ago my wife and I had the privilege of accompanying our daughter, Julaine, as she chose her college wardrobe. I really am not the best judge of style but I could tell as she modeled various dresses, skirts, blouses, and suits that some were modest and some were not! I would give thumbs up or down and Julaine would put the selections on the possibility rack or on the reject rack.

My daughter's willingness to accept my less than perfect judgment has a worthwhile explanation. My wife, Theresa, and I have been married 26 years. I must credit my wife with much of the success in the lives of our children. May I, however, suggest a few reasons for Julaine's compliance to my judgment on her clothes?

Early in her life, I often dated Julaine at local restaurants in Massachusetts and Texas. We also went on special outings together; just the two of us. We would talk about her life and dreams. I gave her complete attention. I would compliment her on every accomplishment of the week or month. I would remind her that although God was most interested with her spiritual development, He was also concerned about how she presented herself and her treatment of other people. I would remind her that God wants our hearts to be pure but He also expects our lifestyle to represent our internal values.

During high school Julaine participated in basketball. Because of a sleep difficulty Julaine's coaches required us to pick her up after every game both home and away. So I made many trips to all corners of our county. What a tremendous opportunity to spend time with the finest young lady I know. It was my privilege to talk to her about her disappointments and joys; her challenges and accomplishments. A difficulty became a fantastic opportunity to spend more time with my daughter.

Years ago Theresa and I bought a purity ring for Julaine. We presented this symbol to Julaine with her full understanding and agreement that she would conduct herself in complete chastity until marriage. We also communicated to her that young women sometimes send messages by the clothes that they wear that conflict with actual moral intent. Wearing a purity ring and then wearing an immodest dress would be unwise: thus the reason for care in her choice of clothes.

Throughout high school Theresa and I would make a fuss over Julaine's wise and modest choices when she would bring clothes home after frugal shopping. When the time came for college clothes I decided to go along! The process took hours -- I mean hours. Okay, I did read some in the car while preliminary choices were made. However, when the time came to make the final judgments, Julaine called Dad.

Some choices were personal, reminding me of Theresa in college. I chose some because of color. I measured each dress, however, by the final standard of modesty. I will never forget that day. Julaine gave me the privilege of participating in what is usually kept from a father. I do believe that dresses, daughters and decency have common ground.

Julaine is now a senior at Baptist Bible College (PA). She is well dressed. We are proud of her. Decency is not determined by clothes, but by the fabric of the soul. That fabric takes a long time to weave.

Dads must invest the threads of time, interest, value, and even some money to develop daughters with character. Dads should realize that symbols like a purity ring, attending basketball games, and approval of dresses are far more important than lectures, rules or being grounded.

Julaine is a tremendous delight and a fine example of decency. Train up a child in the way [she] should go, And when [she] is old [she] will not depart from it. Proverbs 22:6 (NKJV)

Article 11

Chuck & Anna Laws

Eulogy, 2018

Back in the 1990s, Pastor Tim Wilde and I served together in the New York Army National Guard. When he learned that I lived near his parents, he asked if I would visit them. He was concerned about their uncertain relationship with the Lord.

I made my way to their home in the woods which was somewhat of a shrine to "Elvis." They really liked him! I smile as I think of the paintings, the dishes, the memorabilia, etc.

During my first visit I explained the gospel that their son embraced and who also encouraged them to believe. The Lord had prepared their hearts for the message of salvation. When I asked them for a decision to trust Christ, they both responded positively.

I remember kneeling with them in their living room where they both trusted Christ as their personal Savior. The image of them before God is forever etched on my memory.

That was a beginning of my relationship with two very special people.

Immediately they began to attend and ultimately become members of Calvary Baptist Church in Pulaski, New York. I baptized both Chuck and Anna… with her bathing/shower cap is a memory I have not forgotten. (See photo.)

Then they asked if it was alright to invite some friends to also attend. (A pastor's dream for new members!) Seems that they were previously attending a liberal church. And they did invite friends to attend Calvary Baptist: one man is currently a deacon and one lady is the church secretary. Chuck and Anna's influence is still a blessing to CBC.

In early 1997, while discipling Chuck and Anna in their home, he mentioned that they lived on a limited budget and would not be able to give much toward the new facility soon to be built. But then Chuck said, "I might be able help in another way."

At that time in 1997, they were retired and Anna was 67, Chuck was even older. (He served in WWII.) I respectfully asked, "How can you help, Chuck?"

Well, it seems that Chuck was a master electrician. Did he help? Yes, he guided the total wiring of the new 10,000 SF CBC facility.

- *Chuck and Anna became servants when they became Christians!*
- *Chuck and Anna became a blessing to this pastor.*
- *Chuck and Anna left a lasting legacy at Calvary Baptist Church.*
- *Chuck and Anna are now together enjoying their eternal life in Christ.*

Praise the Lord.

Anna Laws, Dr. Ferry, Chuck Laws

Article 12

Blessings on a Bicycle

It has been said, "God never leads us where He won't keep us." This sounds good but it is a concept hard to accept when the rug is pulled out from under us. Such was my situation in 1983 when an emergency surgery put us behind financially. With no personal reserves to tap and tuition due at Dallas Theological Seminary (DTS). I went to school with little hope but firm resolve to register and trust God to provide.

However, I didn't quite have peace about committing to the bill without any means of repaying. So the next day I walked back into the seminary and asked for a withdrawal form. I filled it out and left. As I was leaving I stopped by a large tree on the edge of the parking lot. There the Lord and I had a long talk about His provision or should I say His lack of provision.

I thought about the church family and friends I left behind in Massachusetts so I could attend DTS. I thought about the long all-night grave yard shift working in the machine shop, the afternoon painting job for extra income, and the deer hunting I was missing back home. It was a serious pity party! Yet, I sincerely asked the Lord to provide for my family and for the school bill because I knew He wanted me at DTS.

During this whole conversation with the Lord not one person came or went out of that parking lot. Not a soul was in sight in any direction for probably more than 20 minutes. Then a man on a bicycle caught my attention; coming down Swiss Avenue he entered the parking lot and rode right toward me.

As he approached, I recognized Ed Harris as a transfer student I had befriended and with whom I had completed one class project. Not a close friend but I did know his name and that he had a real love for the Lord.

"How's it going, Allen?" was his greeting.

In a rare moment of transparency, I said, "Truthfully, I am here wrestling with God... expressing my disappointment that I cannot afford to register and yet I know that He wants me here. I'm upset. I've preached, 'God will never lead us where He won't keep us' and yet He seems to have forgotten me. That's how it is going!"

Still straddling his bicycle, my friend asked, "How much is the bill, Allen?"

"$1209," I told him.

Ed then said, "You know, Allen, this week I was awarded a large insurance settlement for the damages to my leg caused by an accident at work last summer. And just last night my wife, Holli and I were asking the Lord in prayer what we should do with the amount we have left over. I think He has just answered our prayer by having us meet here. Go back into the registrar's office and tell him you will have the money here tomorrow morning. I'm thrilled that we met here today, Allen."

I stood there speechless. My heart was in my throat and tears were blurring my vision. Almost questioning my hearing, I asked Ed, "Are you sure you want to do this? What will your wife think? Why me?" His reply was simple, "Why not you? God had you standing here for me to meet. We asked Him last night what we should do with the extra money. God is answering two requests at once: yours and ours. Now, go in there and do it!"

Immediately I did what he said. The check was in my mail box the next morning. My bill was paid in full by an understanding God through a tender servant. The provision did not come through a banker or the lottery or some other big means but the blessing came through a surrendered and generous Christian a bicycle.

And that is a moment to remember.

REVIEW

Reflections of Grace is a compelling testimony to God's grace and faithfulness in the life of my friend Allen Douglas Ferry. God promised Israel in Isaiah 61:3 to give beauty for ashes for His glory. He still does that today. As Doug walked through the ashes of his parents' divorce, his health challenges, and the disappointment of the possibly closed door to chaplaincy, God brought into his life godly men who were instrumental in turning those ashes into beauty. **Reflections of Grace** *is a chronology of the ministry of those men and women in Doug's life that enabled him to touch the lives of so many others.*

My wife and I have known Doug and Theresa for over 50 years. It was my joy to walk beside him in his Chaplaincy ministry and to observe God's hand on their lives from a distance as well as on site visits. From the ashes of Ground Zero and deployments to combat zones, to the ashes of broken lives in correctional institutions, I have observed God using Doug as he helped others turn the ashes of their lives into beauty for God's glory.

I count it a privilege to have Doug as a friend, colleague, and fellow servant.

May the lives referenced in this book challenge us to live for God's glory so that others will see in us Reflections of Grace.

Dr. John B. Murdoch
Director of Chaplaincy Ministries, 1998-2015
General Association of Regular Baptist Churches

REVIEW

I thoroughly enjoyed reading your latest book. It's a privilege to be given a copy to review before it goes to publication.

It's strikes me after reading it how much God loves you, directs you, formed you in your youth, and then used you as His instrument for a wide array of very impressive ministries.

To see the totality of all that you have done and all that God has been for you and done through you is quite the honor. I don't think I can fully express in words how much it meant to me. I am deeply humbled and equally inspired by your book.

Thank you for giving me the honor to look it over.

Dr. Gregory Masiello
Psychologist and Author

REVIEW

REFLECTIONS OF GRACE, invites us into Allen Ferry's unique journey with Jesus Christ. His powerful story reveals, pain, power, purpose and peace wrapped in his human flesh. This life-changing book will capture your attention on every page. His story is shared with a satisfying blend of facing terrifying situations—that most of us avoid—with courage, faith and a gratifying blend of humor. He contrasts his reality with a fantastic gift of humor that sparkles on each page as he brings us back to remembering our amazing Savior Jesus Christ.

Like Dallas Willard's book, **The Allure of Gentleness***, Allen Ferry has lived out the hard questions we all ask about: the problem of evil, the amazing power of Jesus Christ and our freedom of choice. This book is about action and not theory.*

I had the great honor of interacting with Allen when he edited my fourth book. He taught me the gift of laughter. He had a Mac and I had an PC. From this perspective and our vastly different backgrounds, we found a common ground: a deep respect and gratitude for one of our favorite professors, and authors, Howard Hendricks. It was an honor that Allen agreed to patiently help me.

I consider Allen Ferry a great friend and a gracious servant of our Lord Jesus Christ and his wonderful family, Theresa, Julaine and Enoch are great blessings to all that know them.

You will want to read this book again and again. I plan to buy copies for my children.

Jane Ann Derr
Widow, mother, grandmother, great-grandmother, missionary in Ghana, West Africa & author

REVIEW

This is the chronicle of a man who has been there, done that, and indeed does have the tee shirts—lots of them.

From happy child to disappointed teen to young pastor and to a now retired pastor/chaplain/colonel, this is a quick overview of the men and women who have had a bit of influence and the way in which they exerted that influence. The over-riding theme is that these folks, who sought only to show the love of their Savior, exerted so much influence on this one man. So many went to their Heavenly home without knowing all that would be accomplished for the Kingdom as a result of what they had poured into this one man.

As Allen writes, we see the guiding Hand of the Almighty clearly shown in the people and circumstances that placed in his path.

As you read this, be guided by the lesson that what you do, whom you befriend, how you handle issues all may have impact far beyond all that you may know in your life.

Reverend Bill Pitcher
Pastor, First Baptist Church
Amsterdam, New York

REVIEW

This memoir is a heartwarming recollection of the author's remarkable life. It is a journey steeped in faith and fashioned by God in unexpected and miraculous ways. It is a must-read reminder that God is in control even as the author takes us through his parents' divorce, his cancer, military deployment, and the inevitable challenges of chaplaincy.

Real people are honored by tribute, and readers mount the motorcycle of mortality hanging on to their helmets on a ride that ultimately teaches us we are only human.

A true testimony to God's goodness, this book reflects a soft spirit of humility, gentle humor and the tender victory of commitment to Christ.

Dr. Hyacinth Byron-Cox
Former Professor at Monroe College
Ph.D., Psychology

THE BEGINNING

Reflections of Grace is much more than my story. It is the account of the amazing power of personal influence… the people who influenced and invested in me.

Now, it is your turn.

Made in the USA
Monee, IL
05 November 2024

69414658R00125